THE POLITICAL CONTEXT OF SOCIOLOGY

BY LEON BRAMSON

PRINCETON, NEW JERSEY
PRINCETON UNIVERSITY PRESS

Publication of this book has been aided
by the Ford Foundation program to support publication,
through university presses, of work in
the humanities and social sciences.

First Princeton Paperback Printing, 1967
Fourth Printing, 1974

PRINTED IN THE UNITED STATES OF AMERICA
BY PRINCETON UNIVERSITY PRESS, PRINCETON, NEW JERSEY

SBEN 14369264 10-7-2014

PREFACE

THIS book represents an attempt to grapple with the problem of the influence of social and political theories on the practice of sociology. It is quite limited in scope and has three parts. In the first I have explored some of the historical uses of sociology, using material from the 19th century when evidence of such influence was much more obvious than it is today. I have tried to distinguish between sociologies of conservation and change, paradoxically maintaining that in spite of such differences, sociology is intrinsically biased in its emphasis on social order, an emphasis which transcends political labelling of the "Left-Right" variety. The rise of European sociology in the 19th century is discussed in terms of conservation and change with reference to the concepts of the mass and mass society.

In the second part, I have shown how these concepts were received by American sociologists functioning within a liberal milieu. Comparing European and American studies of the crowd, I have told how a distinctively American theory of collective behavior arose, within which was developed a concept of mass behavior. In showing how liberal American sociologists tried to cope with conservative and even reactionary implications in theories of the crowd and the mass without compromising their liberalism, I have also explored some aspects of American sociology itself. This exploration provides a kind of case study in the influence of a social and political milieu on the presuppositions and implications of theory and research. To illustrate this I examined American research on mass communications and discussed some of the ideological ambiguities resulting from the importation of the mass concept to the United States.

Finally, in the third part, I examined the ideological background of contemporary theorists of mass society, and raised some questions about the notion that mass culture leads to totalitarianism. I then tried to assess the methodological implications of this material for the practice of social research.

This study is not exhaustive: it does not deal with all uses of the mass concept as currently employed by social scientists. It does not deal at great length with the theory of mass society in explaining political phenomena, nor does it try to assess this theory in the light of changes in Western institutions in the last century. I have chosen to be selective in fulfilling my purpose: the examination of the evolution of a single set of ideas, to see how the work of sociologists has been influenced by social and political thought. There may be much to learn about the history and method of the discipline from such an attempt, however rudimentary.

That there is a methodological moral to the study will be clear to the reader if he has the patience to follow my argument, with its turns and digressions, to the end. He will find the conviction that a naïve positivism no longer represents a useful methodological approach for sociologists, if it ever did, and that subjective elements in social science research and conceptualization are not only inevitable but desirable. The fact that this idea is not original should not detract from its importance. Some truths will bear repeating, especially in American sociology with its severe discontinuities. But it is also true that it is easier to criticize the noble dream of a value-free social science than to create a workable alternative which does not degenerate into irrationalism. Whether or not this is possible I regard as an open question, but I believe that it is better for sociology that it be open than closed with the rusty padlock of dogmatic positivism.

This book was in its original form a doctoral dissertation at Harvard University. That it should retain an academic air is inevitable. I have not made extensive revisions; rather, I decided to present my study more or less as it stood in November 1958, when I completed it. Since that time several books have been published which bear on the questions taken up here. Most important of these in relation to this book is

Preface

probably William Kornhauser's *The Politics of Mass Society*
(Glencoe: Free Press, 1959), which provides an excellent
guide to the sociological literature on the subject and a judi-
cious (and possibly definitive) assessment of the mass society
concept in the explanation of political behavior. I will leave
to the reader the resolution of any differences he may find
between Professor Kornhauser's approach to the theory of
mass society and mine. On the institutional aspects of mass
society theory in the United States, *The Eclipse of Community*
(Princeton: Princeton University Press, 1960) by Maurice R.
Stein may be quite helpful. As a general study of the influence
of American values on what the author regards as a distinctively American discipline, Bernard Crick's *The American
Science of Politics* (California: University of California Press,
1959) represents a piece of admirable, if sometimes querulous,
critical analysis. Finally, both H. Stuart Hughes's *Consciousness and Society: The Reorientation of European Social
Thought, 1890-1930* (New York: Knopf, 1958) and Phillip
Rieff's *Freud: The Mind of the Moralist* (New York: Viking,
1959) strike me as models for any one interested in the study
of the social sciences as intellectual history.

Many of the ideas in this book were developed in an unpublished paper, "The Concept of the Mass," during my first
winter of graduate study in sociology at the University of
Chicago in 1950-1951. After a long period of incubation during
military service and further study of social and political
thought, I finally returned to this theme in my dissertation.
A Fulbright scholarship to the Netherlands in 1957-1958
enabled me to think through the problem once more and to
write the first draft. I am very grateful to the members of the
graduate seminar in sociology at the University of Nijmegen
who heard me present these ideas and who subjected them
to patient criticism. Professor A. Oldendorff, now of the Technical Institute at Eindhoven, was the first to read the manuscript, and I am indebted to him for encouragement and
critical comment. The seminar would not have been possible

and my stay in the Netherlands would have been far less pleasant without the help of Professor Oldendorff, Dr. Jan Thurlings of the University of Nijmegen and Dr. Johanna J. van Dullemen of the U.S. Educational Foundation in The Hague. The staff of the library of the Sociological Seminar of the University of Amsterdam were extremely helpful, especially Miss W. Fetlaar. The following persons read the manuscript or parts of it and offered comments which were in all cases most helpful: Dr. Jeremy Azrael, Dr. Joel H. Feigon, Professor H. Stuart Hughes, M. H. Reeves, Professor David Riesman and Dr. Michael Weinberg.

To my thesis advisors, Professor Louis Hartz and Dr. Barrington Moore, Jr. of Harvard University, I owe a special debt of gratitude for their encouragement and painstaking criticism. To Professor Daniel Bell I owe the special thanks that are due a stimulating teacher and friend. And I wish to acknowledge here my debts to my other teachers at the University of Chicago, especially Professors Everett C. Hughes, David Riesman (now at Harvard), Tamotsu Shibutani (now at California), and Alan Gewirth; and to Professors Hartz, Moore, Crane Brinton and Morton G. White at Harvard University. Few men have been more fortunate than I in their teachers. Let none of those mentioned above be held responsible for my mistakes.

Finally, I wish to thank my mother and father, whose help and encouragement were decisive at every phase of the writing.

April 9, 1960
Cambridge, Mass.

PREFACE TO THE SECOND PRINTING

To bring this book up to date, to take account of the many excellent criticisms of it which fellow scholars have made, would entail rewriting it completely. I confess that this task holds little appeal for me. Having slain this particular tiger once, it would be perverse to yearn for visits to the tiger's cage at the zoo. The desires of the Princeton University Press to reproduce the book by photo-offset process called for a minimum of changes and coincided with my own predilections. The result is that I have not changed it at all.

I cannot avoid, however, the following observations which might help to correct certain emphases in the text:

(1) A notorious defect of individualist liberalism is its failure to take account of the degree to which any true individuality is shaped within a web of interpersonal relationships;

(2) Methodological problems discussed in the book (such as the disguising of value judgments as facts) are more frequently encountered in the study of human communities by sociologists and anthropologists than in demographic studies or small-group experiments.

Since this study was written, a number of works have come to my attention which, in my opinion, strengthen its central theses. An expanded version of the book would certainly contain sections on the sociology of work and the sociology of the city, and would rely on the insights provided in the research and theory exemplified in the following citations:

Blauner, Robert. "Work Satisfaction and Industrial Trends in Modern Society," *Labor and Trade Unionism*, eds. W. Galenson and S. M. Lipset, New York: Wiley, 1960.

Greer, Scott. "Individual Participation in Mass Society," *Approaches to the Study of Politics*, ed. R. Young, Evanston: Northwestern University Press, 1958.

Gans, Herbert. "Urbanism and Suburbanism as Ways of Life: A Re-evaluation of Definitions," *Human Behavior and Social Processes*, ed. A. M. Rose, Boston: Houghton Mifflin, 1962.

With regard to the methodological issues raised here, two additional references are relevant:

Gouldner, Alvin. "Anti-Minotaur: The Myth of a Value-Free Sociology," *Social Problems*, Winter, 1962.
Shils, Edward. "The Calling of Sociology," *Theories of Society*, ed. T. Parsons, et al., Vol. II, New York: Free Press, 1962.

Finally, I am also obliged to admit that if Mary Elizabeth Bramson had been able to edit the original, there is no question that this printing would be more readable than it is at the present time.

L B

September 1966

ACKNOWLEDGMENTS

THE following authors and publishers have kindly granted me permission to quote passages from their publications:

Appleton-Century-Crofts, Inc., New York; "The Scientific World-Perspective," by Kasimir Adjukiewicz, in H. Feigl and W. Sellars, *Readings in Philosophical Analysis*, copyright 1949.

Beacon Press, Inc., Boston, for *Eros and Civilization*, by Herbert Marcuse, copyright 1955.

Commentary, and The American Jewish Committee, for "The Theory of Mass Society," by Daniel Bell, copyright 1956.

Harper and Brothers, New York, for *An American Dilemma*, by Gunnar Myrdal, copyright 1944.

Henry Holt and Company, Inc. (Dryden Press), New York, for "Social Disorganization," by Don Martindale, in H. Becker and A. Boskoff, *Modern Sociological Theory*, copyright 1957.

Alfred A. Knopf, Inc., New York, for *The Age of Reform*, by Richard Hofstadter, copyright 1955.

Oxford University Press, Inc., New York, for *Essays on Sociology and Social Psychology*, by Karl Mannheim, copyright 1953.

Partisan Review for "Liberalism, Conservatism and the Babel of Tongues," by Cushing Strout, copyright 1958.

Philosophical Library, New York, for "American Sociology," by Robert E. L. Faris, in G. Gurvitch and W. E. Moore, *Twentieth Century Sociology*, copyright 1945.

Random House, Inc., New York (Doubleday and Company), for The Development of Modern Sociology, by Roscoe C. Hinkle and Gisela J. Hinkle, copyright 1954.

The American Sociological Association, for "Moulding of Mass Behavior Through the Motion Pictures," *Publications of the American Sociological Society*, by Herbert Blumer, copyright 1935.

Acknowledgments

The Free Press, Inc., Glencoe, Illinois for "Social Stratification and Political Power," by Reinhard Bendix, in *Class, Status and Power*, copyright 1953.

The Sewanee Review for "Daydreams and Nightmares: Reflections on the Criticism of Mass Culture," by Edward A. Shils, copyright 1957.

The University of Chicago Press, for "American Sociology, 1915-1947," by Louis Wirth, in the Index to Vol. 1-52. *American Journal of Sociology*, copyright 1947 by the University of Chicago; and for "Report on an Educational Campaign: The Cincinnati Plan for the United Nations," by Shirley A. Star and Helen MacGill Hughes, *American Journal of Sociology*, copyright 1950 by the University of Chicago.

The Wilhelm Reich Infant Trust Fund, for *The Mass Psychology of Fascism* by Wilhelm Reich, copyright 1946.

CONTENTS

THE

POLITICAL CONTEXT

OF SOCIOLOGY

INTRODUCTION

THE sociological impulse had many origins, but it was most often expressed in the belief that there were laws of human behavior, in some sense analogous to the laws of Newtonian physics. Not only were these laws held to be discoverable by men, but their discovery was deemed desirable, chiefly because such laws could be useful to men in controlling the social world, in somewhat the same way that Newtonian physics had proved useful in the physical and material world. Today this ideal seems much further away than it did in the 19th century. Comte's social physics has never been able to command the respect accorded to Newton's. In the middle of the 20th century social scientists are still awaiting their Newton, not to speak of their Einstein; and some among their number, perhaps reflecting the chastened optimism of their time, have declared that there are good reasons to believe that he will never appear: "The precise form that social systems will take will obviously depend upon the detailed series of events of which they are the outcome at any given moment of history. The function of social theory in the field of historical change is not to prophesy the future but rather to work out the limitations within which future developments are likely to occur."[1]

The general name given to such reflections in the social sciences is methodology; and an awareness of methodological problems will, I hope, be diffused throughout this study. This is necessary because of the character of the problem; it

---

[1] W. H. J. Sprott, *Science and Social Action* (Glencoe: Free Press, 1956), p. 140. Cf. also John Madge, *The Tools of Social Science* (London: Longmans, 1953), Ch. 6; Robert Redfield, *The Primitive World and Its Transformations* (Ithaca: Cornell University Press, 1953), pp. 163-165; Joseph Kahl, *The American Class Structure* (New York: Rinehart, 1956), p. 47; Pitirim Sorokin, *Fads and Foibles of Social Science* (Chicago: Regnery Pub. Co., 1956); Nathan Glazer, "The American Soldier as Science," *Commentary*, Vol. 8, No. 5, November, 1949; William H. Whyte, Jr., *The Organization Man* (New York: Doubleday Anchor, 1957), Part I, Ch. 3, Part IV; Herbert Blumer, "What is Wrong With Social Theory," *American Sociological Review*, Vol. 1, No. 19, February 1954, pp. 3-10.

should become clear that I am trying to take a double view of sociology: that from within, and also that from without. Sociology is not some Baconian infusion of dry light; it is part of the cultural context from which it springs. To overlook this would be to overlook the possibilities of sociology as a source for the intellectual historian, not to mention the character of the sociological enterprise itself.

This means that the activities of sociologists may become the data for the analyst of the history of ideas; and that the results of such inquiry will have relevance, not only for history, but for sociology itself. But there are difficulties here, and one must exercise great care: "The history of ideas cannot be written like an invoice of standardized goods. It is a subject requiring infinite tact. On the one hand, diversity must be reduced to clear patterns for the sake of intelligibility; and on the other, the meaning of each idea must be preserved from falsification by constant reference to its place and purport in history."[2]

This advice, applied so well to the idea of romanticism by Professor Barzun, could provide some guidance in considering the concept of mass society. Simply because people use the same word for something is no indication that they mean the same thing; this platitude is one of those frequently ignored by sociologists, who, increasingly accustomed to methodological agony, are becoming more aware of such problems. It is not as easy as it used to be to find articles in the learned journals in which a man who has made a study of class in America will go ahead to make easy comparisons with class in Europe, the ahistorical tradition of his discipline leading him to assume that he is talking about the same thing in both instances.[3] Yet what could be easier than to commit this error in the study of

---

[2] Jacques Barzun, *Romanticism and the Modern Ego* (Boston: Little, Brown, 1954), p. 15.

[3] See Arnold M. Rose, "The Concept of Class and American Sociology," *Social Research*, Vol. 25, No. 1, Spring 1958, pp. 53-69. I may have exhibited some of the same rigidities in connection with the concept of liberalism in the chapters that follow.

"mass society," a concept so utterly banal, so much a sociological commonplace of textbooks on social disorganization, as almost to defy analysis?

A cautionary note may be in order: awareness of methodological problems does not mean that they can be solved. They may, indeed, be insoluble. Many men have reasoned that since one can become aware of a "problem," one can guard against it or solve it or somehow do both. This is not necessarily so.[4]

This study is at the same time an inquiry into the influence of social and political philosophies on sociological theories, and an assessment of sociological work in a specific area. I will try to show that within a specific social and political context, that of post-Revolutionary Europe, a number of ideas take shape and ultimately culminate in a theory of "mass society." The concept is accepted by most European sociologists who employ it as being a "scientific" one. American sociologists, within a different social and political context, subject this idea to a subtle transformation. They come to speak of similar subject matter in a completely different way. They give it a decisive theoretical twist, a different interpretation. But they, too, claim the mantle of science. It is as if there were two different versions of the periodic table, one for each side of the Atlantic. But sociology is not chemistry; perhaps it is more like poetry. And perhaps this is why a description of this effort as a contribution to the sociology of knowledge does not satisfy me. Such a description implies that this study has significance within a larger context, and that given the

---

[4] But this brings out an interesting difference of vocabulary between Europeans and Americans, a difference which may symbolize some of the issues discussed in this essay. For it is often the case that Americans, when they speak of a "problem," imply that it is something that can eventually be solved. John Dewey is partially responsible for this, with his social psychology which begins with a "problematic situation." There is also our activist tradition and our now much belabored optimism. But when Europeans speak of "problems," they are often thinking of something which cannot be solved at all; and this is sometimes revealed in their subsequent discourse. Conventions of discourse like this one may occasionally provide illumination in the darkness we call the history of ideas.

same historical conditions, the same kinds of things will happen. Unfortunately, there is no way to test such an assertion in any precise way. Historical conditions are never the same; and there will not even be a similar set of conditions, in the sense of there being the same forces at work. (Sociologists habitually use imagery derived from physics, thereby combining an obeisance and a fond hope.) In the laboratory we may arrange an experiment, and our descriptions may involve use of the phrase, "other conditions being equal." But conditions never are equal outside the laboratory. The British, the French, the Russians and the Americans have all had something happen which historians call a "revolution." Valiant efforts to construct a sociology of revolution on the basis of these examples have failed, if the test of success is the development of a predictive instrument.[5]

But I do not want to stress the limitations of sociology without putting in a word about its possibilities. Sociology does not have to provide exact predictions in order to be useful; it can tell us something about the future, perhaps by narrowing the range of alternatives on the basis of knowledge of the past: "Where the nature of the processes is properly understood, analysis can proceed toward outlining the range of possibilities for the future and the costs of alternative policies. We need not be deterred by the impossibility of precise prediction for relationships that are not completely determinate. The sociologist has added unnecessarily to his sense of professional inadequacy by feeling compelled to predict the inevitable outcome of any situation."[6]

If a sociologist (or a daring historian *incognito*) tries to develop a set of characteristics or classes of events or phases which may obtain in the case of every revolution—that is, a list of the events which he has found all revolutions to have

[5] See, for example, Crane Brinton, *The Anatomy of Revolution* (New York: Prentice-Hall, 1938).

[6] Barrington Moore, Jr., "Sociological Theory and Contemporary Politics," *American Journal of Sociology*, Vol. 61, No. 2, September 1955, p. 115.

in common—at the end of this process he will know more about "revolutions" than when he began, although he may not have produced a predictive instrument. He may indeed be able to point out significant recurrences, knowledge of which may be useful in dealing with present or future problems. He may heighten our expectation that given certain broad conditions, certain events might ensue. That this represents a retreat from the proud claims of the 19th century science of man, I have already indicated. But we should not be put off by the touch of melancholy here. The redefinition and modification of that old dream of a social science is not yet finished. I will try to contribute to that redefinition in the last chapter of this book, when I take up the problems raised by the disguising of value judgments as facts, and try to suggest how the thoughtful social scientist might cope with them.

For better or for worse, then, this essay will be informed by a split consciousness: that of the sociologist examining the state of his discipline with respect to a specific problem, and that of the historian of ideas trying to assess the influence of political and social philosophies on sociological theory. At any given point the perspective of one or the other will be predominant; the reader will require a keen eye for context. The ambiguity of such a method, it is hoped, will not affect its potential usefulness in the drive toward intellectual self-awareness, which is the characteristic obligation of our time.[7]

[7] Cf. H. Stuart Hughes, *Consciousness and Society: The Reorientation of European Social Thought, 1890-1930* (New York: Knopf, 1958).

PART ONE

CHAPTER ONE

THE USES OF SOCIOLOGY

THE study of 19th century sociology is rewarding, in that so many of the problems which plague thoughtful social scientists were then in some ways more well-defined. The sociological idea was taken up with enthusiasm by men of imagination who were inspired by the victorious application of the scientific method to the conquest of physical nature. But modern sociology begins with men who had somewhat different perspectives: the European conservatives of the last decade of the 18th and first decades of the 19th century. These thinkers, men like Hegel, Comte, Bonald and de Maistre, shared a concern with the study of human society—with what Louis Wirth later described in his definition of sociology as "that which is true of human beings by virtue of the fact that they everywhere live a collective life." Yet, while sharing an interest in such inquiry, they entertained quite different notions of its purposes. Agreeing on the desirability of the study of the laws of group life, they differed considerably in their view of the uses of such study.

These various thinkers conceived of the purpose of their sociology in terms of different kinds of social and political philosophies. Such philosophies found their way into sociology, implicitly or explicitly, with the result that certain characteristic concepts and frames of reference developed in conjunction with the rise of sociology itself. A distinction should be made, however, between the overt or covert influence on sociology of social and political theories, and a kind of bias which may be intrinsic to the sociological enterprise. The latter type of bias, I believe, is best expressed in the concept of *order*. I do not mean here merely the idea of the uniformity of nature, a faith which characterized much of 18th century scientific thought.[1]

[1] Cf. Alfred North Whitehead, *Science and the Modern World* (New York: Mentor, 1949), Ch. 1; and Carl Becker, *The Heavenly City of the 18th Century Philosophers* (New Haven: Yale University Press, 1938).

I refer to the ideal of social order, the sociological focus on the group rather than the individual, a legacy from sociology's most important historical source, 19th century European conservatism.[2]

Now the sociological idea is a complex one, and represents a mixture of many faiths and theories. The strains of natural law, science, materialism, determinism and inevitability, the romantic emphasis on organic wholes and on conflict, ideas of progress and evolution, all have found their way into its intellectual pedigree. It emerged in striking form in the period of reaction following the French Revolution as an antidote to the idealism of many Enlightenment philosophers.[3] Although there were differences among the generations of Enlightenment theorists, in the field of social theory the individualistic and rationalistic emphases of Locke may be said to have ruled the field after being imported to France and translated, with suitable changes, into a doctrine more congenial to the *philosophes*. The result may be seen in the broad movement toward the application of "reason" in human affairs—often in the direction of a limitation of government control over industry and commerce—and also in the general environmentalist theory which asserted the great plasticity of individuals

[2] See F. A. Hayek, *The Counter-Revolution of Science* (Glencoe: Free Press, 1952); Albert Salomon, *The Tyranny of Progress* (New York: Noonday Press, 1955).

A European sociologist who had emigrated to the United States took his American colleagues to task not so long ago for "forgetting" this: "Contrary to a popular opinion which identifies sociology with the practical discipline of social welfare, our science has an eminently political origin. Today it is almost forgotten that Saint Simon, Auguste Comte, and Lorenz Stein conceived the new science of society as an antidote against the poison of social disintegration which, in their opinion, had taken effect since the turn of the 18th [*sic*] century, if not much earlier." Rudolf Heberle, "On Political Ecology," *Social Forces*, Vol. 31, No. 1, October 1952.

[3] "In the impact of the Revolution upon the traditional social group may be seen much of the effective social background of the rise of sociology in France. Historically, sociology in its systematic form rests upon the concept of the social group and the problem of social disorganization." Robert A. Nisbet, "The French Revolution and the Rise of Sociology," *American Journal of Sociology*, Vol. 49, No. 2, September 1943, p. 160. I am indebted to Prof. Nisbet's discussion of this problem in his excellent study, *The Quest For Community* (New York: Oxford University Press, 1953).

and institutions, the perfectibility of the individual man considered apart from his social context. These dusty but familiar ideas were the common property of a large number of 18th century thinkers whom we think of as men of the Enlightenment.

The French conservatives of the early 19th century denounced the individualism of these theorists and their strictures against divine-right monarchy, aristocracy and Church. The attempt to put these theories into practice, they said, had destroyed the social fabric, separated men from one another, and created individualistic atoms floating helplessly in an anarchic void. The restoration of social order was the preoccupation not only of Bonald and de Maistre,[4] but also of Comte, the father of sociology.[5]

Many of the key concepts of sociology illustrate this concern with the maintenance and conservation of order; ideas such as status, hierarchy, ritual, integration, social function and social control are themselves a part of the history of the

[4] *Étude sur la souveraineté, Oeuvres inédites* (Paris: Vaton Fréres 1870); "Du Pape," *Oeuvres* (Brussels: Société Nationale Pour la Propagation des Bon Livres, 1838). The author of a recent essay on de Maistre declares that Bonald and de Maistre "each had the same conservative purpose behind his sociology." M. Kramer, "History in the Mind of Joseph de Maistre," Department of History, Harvard University, 1954.

[5] Cf. especially Auguste Comte, *Essays* (London: G. Routledge and Sons, 1911), pp. 88, 96-98, 292-95; "Plan of the Scientific Operations Necessary for the Regeneration of Society," *System of Positive Polity* (London: Longmans, 1875-77), Vol. IV, Appendix III, pp. 527-89 (especially the statements on p. 560); and the "General View of Positivism," *System of Positive Polity*, Vol. I. Although he is often acknowledged as the "father" of the discipline, American sociologists have usually neglected the reactionary aspects of Comte's thought, his hostility to the Enlightenment and the French Revolution. This was seen quite clearly by the later Mill, however, who declared: "And some of those modern reformers who have placed themselves in strongest opposition to the religions of the past, have been no way behind either churches or sects in their assertion of the right of spiritual domination: M. Comte, in particular, whose social system, as unfolded in his *Systeme de politique positive*, aims at establishing (though by moral more than by legal appliances) a despotism of society over the individual surpassing anything contemplated in the political ideal of the most rigid disciplinarian among the ancient philosophers." J. S. Mill, "On Liberty," *Utilitarianism, Liberty and Representative Government* (New York: Dutton, 1951), p. 101.

reaction to the ideals of the French Revolution: individualism, secularism, scientific rationalism, and egalitarianism.[6] What conservative critics saw as resulting from these movements was not the progressive liberation of individuals, but increasing insecurity and alienation, the breakdown of traditional associations and group ties. The view of society and human nature developed by such conservative thinkers as Burke, Bonald, de Maistre and, to some extent Hegel, was in fact quite opposed to the view of the rationalists and individualists such as Locke, Voltaire, and Bentham. Society for the conservatives was an organic entity, not a mere aggregate of individuals capable of manipulation by the man with a blueprint for a new order. The delicate balance of society is a product of the working out of history: social forms have roots in the past, and are not mere artifacts. Who will not recognize the similarity between Durkheim's claim for the metaphysical reality of the group and Burke's partnership of the dead, the living, and the unborn?

In the conservative view, society is primary to the individual, from an historical, logical, and ethical standpoint. The individual as we know him can never come into existence without society, without the influence of what contemporary sociologists call "the socialization process." When modern sociologists tell us that without society there is no communication (Mead), no language (Sapir), no morality and no emotional development (Cooley), they are echoing the arguments of the embattled French conservatives cited above. Indeed, both groups of theorists tell us that only through society does the individual become a "human being." The 19th century conservatives argued that the unity of society cannot be arbitrarily broken down into atomized and abstract individuals, even for purposes of political theory. Even individuality, they declared, is social, nurtured within the context of a group of like-minded individuals. Clearly this view is not unrelated to current sociological research on small groups and

[6] Robert A. Nisbet, "Conservatism and Sociology," *American Journal of Sociology*, Vol. 58, No. 2, September 1952.

the so-called "rediscovery of the primary group." For the French conservatives, however, these small groups and associations standing between the atomized individual and an omnipotent state formed the main bastion of social and political liberty. From such considerations is derived the political theory of pluralism.

The conservative image of society also stresses interdependence, the relationships between the parts of a system that is somehow more than merely the sum of those parts (Hegel). Thus there are interconnections between customs, habits, institutions; and attempts to alter one aspect of the complex social organism will affect all the other parts as well. The organic analogy, even though it was used by liberals like Herbert Spencer, is potentially a conservative concept. All the parts of the social whole are responses to basic, fixed human needs, so that every custom, every artifact, every social web has the purpose of binding discrete human individuals into a social unity. Every folk belief, no matter how ludicrous or outmoded it might seem to the enlightened, is a product of the past and has its purpose in providing "emotional cement." It is in the context of small groups, the family, the local community, the occupational associations, the religious groups, that men find the necessary support for their emotional existence. Abstractions, rationality, impersonal relations will not suffice to hold a society together. Here, in fact, among the conservatives of the early 19th century, it is not difficult to see the beginnings of a theory of mass society. For in the conservative view the weakening and dislocation of traditional ties results in the creation of a mass of alienated and isolated individual atoms, an easy mark for the demagogue offering political panaceas for salvation in this world.

It was in similar terms that the French conservatives in particular attacked religious individualism. Protestantism itself could only lead to social disorganization, since it tended to ignore the historic, ritualistic and symbolic elements in religion in its attack on the Roman Church.

Society itself exists through ritual, worship and ceremony; and without its sacred aspect, it will not hold together. Hierarchy, superordination and subordination, a definite status within the social order, are all necessary for social cohesion. Pre-rational beliefs and habits, not "reason," are the foundation of legitimate authority. Hierarchy and authority are not degrading in their effect on the individual; they reinforce consensus and protect the individual from himself. They give him a sense of place in an ordered world. Force and violence, not "irrationality" of supposedly outmoded institutions, are degrading; and they are the inevitable result of the dissolution of the normal patterns of authority.

I do not mean to imply here that the influence of these conservative ideas on sociological theory impugns the validity of that theory. Nor do I mean to indicate that there is no difference between present-day sociology and European conservatism of the early 19th century. I do wish to stress the idea that although sociology has many potential uses and has been enlisted in support of various political faiths, it is by the nature of its key concepts and approaches intrinsically oriented toward the group rather than the individual, toward the herd rather than the lone stray. In connection with this emphasis, sociology stresses the notions of order, of collectivity, of social organization, irrespective of political labels such as "Left" or "Right." Thus sociology has an anti-liberal twist, and may even be considered as a critique of the traditional liberal ideal of individualism.[7] Now it is true that individual liberty can take firm root and come to flower only in the soil

[7] By "liberal" here and elsewhere in this book I intend the classical doctrine of political and economic individualism, with its emphasis on rationality, equality, religious liberty, constitutionalism, majority rule and natural rights. Associated socially and culturally with middle-class hegemony, it has emphasized self-mastery, self-reliance, achievement, an orientation toward the future and, above all, individuality. It should be clear that I do not intend the contemporary American usage which indicates sympathy with democratic socialism and trade unionism, but the accepted 19th century use of the term.

of a social order where individual rights are guaranteed by law and custom. I do not intend to minimize the importance of such a social order, nor to imply that the individual should be seen in isolation from his society. Yet few sociologists have been distinguished by their concern for the individual as opposed to their preoccupation with social disintegration. A consideration of the anti-liberal aspect of sociology brings into sharp relief the links between a reactionary like de Maistre, who idealized the feudal order, and a radical like Marx, who visualized a new industrial order. Neither Marx nor de Maistre was an individualist.[8] A sociologist who is also a liberal-individualist, then, may encounter theoretical difficulties and contradictions. Sociological concepts, with their load of anti-liberal freight derived from European social and political philosophies, undergo a subtle transformation at the hands of American sociologists when imported into the liberal American context. Or, with perhaps equal frequency, these concepts are uncritically applied to the American realities without regard for the deficiencies of the resulting analysis.[9] The tension between these sociological concepts and the liberalism of many American sociologists appears dramatically in the works of such men as Robert Ezra Park and other members of the German-influenced Chicago school of sociology. This much-neglected aspect of American intellectual history will be treated in somewhat more detail in Chapters Three and Four.

Now I have said that although men may agree on the desirability of the study of group life, they may differ considerably in their views of the uses and purposes of such study. A review of these differences prompts me to make a broad and necessarily vague distinction between sociologies of con-

[8] Despite Marx's well-known statement to the contrary in *The German Ideology* (New York: International Publishers, 1947), p. 22, the emphasis on class, class-consciousness and collective control precludes the possibility of an individualistic doctrine in the classical sense cited above.

[9] Examples are legion; cf. Arnold M. Rose, "The Concept of Class and American Sociology," *Social Research*, Vol. 25, No. 1, Spring 1958.

servation and equilibrium on the one hand and sociologies of change and process on the other.[10] I mean to emphasize nothing more than that some sociologies, by virtue of their leading concepts, the problems they characteristically attack and their basic presuppositions, are better suited for the analysis of order, equilibrium, stability and the persistence of social patterns; and that other sociologies, by virtue of their particular characteristics, seem better fitted for the study of process, change, development and dynamics. These two sociologies are not mutually exclusive; I do not intend absolutely airtight categories, but only heuristic constructs to help bring out the relation between these movements of thought in the 19th and 20th centuries.

There may be an objection at this point: has not the zeal for classification itself led to a subtle contradiction? If all sociology, irrespective of the social and political faith which animates it, and regardless of the ends for which it has been devised, leans theoretically in the direction of social order, organization, cohesion and groupness, how is it possible that there should be a sociology of change? The answer, I think, is that the sociology of change as described above is also infected with this bias; but that it has usually been devised by men interested in a *re*-organization of society, a change in the *status quo*, the foundation of a *new* order, or as it has frequently been expressed, "social reconstruction." The rhetoric of reconstruction is found in sociologies of both the Left and the Right. This rhetoric emphasizes, although from different standpoints in the two cases, the follies, excesses and deficiencies of liberalism.

There is another aspect of the concept of order in relation to the two sociologies which will bear some attention. I refer not to the emphasis on social organization, but to the notion of the uniformity of nature mentioned previously. Both the

[10] See Barrington Moore Jr., "Sociological Theory and Contemporary Politics," *American Journal of Sociology*, Vol. 61, No. 2, 1955. I am indebted to Dr. Moore for his suggestive distinction between the theories of equilibrium and process.

sociology of conservation and the sociology of change have reference to a concept of "natural order"; hence we must explore the ambiguities of the concept of *natural law* in terms of which this natural order is usually expressed.[11] There are, broadly speaking, two traditions of natural law that become persistently intertwined during this period: the idea of such physical laws of nature as the Newtonian inverse square law; and the ethical tradition of natural law, so important in Christian thought and subsequently in modern political theory. The ambiguity of the concept of natural law resulted in two persistent confusions of the idea by its exponents: they either invested the physical laws of nature with moral qualities, or identified moral and ethical imperatives with the characteristics of physical laws of nature. The first confusion of the natural law concept is characteristic of the sociology of change; the second is usually associated with the sociology of conservation.

To take the sociology of conservation first: I have indicated that thinkers like Bonald and de Maistre tried to show the limitations of the individualistic ideals of the Enlightenment theorists, and that they proclaimed the dependence of men on a structured group life—a hierarchical social order in which each is assured of his status. The absence of such a social order was for them the beginning of social chaos. Their views, decisive for much later sociology, were quite pessimistic: they prided themselves on a "realistic" image of human nature. In sociological language, they were more interested in ascription than in achievement, more sensitized to security than to aspiration. Their sociology of conservation, emphasizing the persistence of institutions, equilibrium, social statics rather than social dynamics, was announced as resting on *natural laws*. That is, these thinkers endowed the social hierarchy which they studied with ethical qualities. They tried to give ethical sanction to social facts by discussing those facts as the result of the working out of laws of nature. Thus they ended, like

[11] I am indebted to Prof. Louis Hartz for his analysis of the ambiguities of the natural law concept in the following discussion.

some contemporary "functionalists," by stressing the "inevitable" place of certain institutions in a natural order of society: structure and hierarchy, the crown and the altar, are both inevitable concomitants of social existence and the most desirable institutional arrangement.

This theoretical maneuver is exactly the reverse of that carried out by the sociologists of change, whose roots in this respect spring in part from the individualistic philosophers of the Enlightenment. These philosophers were involved in the same confusion generated by the natural law concept, but the roles of fact and value were reversed. The values of the Enlightenment rather than the facts of the existing institutional structure became the focus of attention: the ideal of the infinitely perfectible and rational individual freed from pernicious group influences, harmoniously interacting with others like him for the inevitable good of the whole. Instead of endowing the facts of the existing order with ethical sanctions, these thinkers were concerned with showing that the ideals they championed were in fact "natural rights" or laws of nature that must be obeyed. This conception of natural law, with its idealized image of Man freed from the economic, social, political and religious restrictions of the old order, contrasted sharply with the "natural laws" of the French conservatives.

But the sociology of change, of process, did not come into existence with the 18th century philosophers. Rather, it followed upon the formulation of a sociology of conservation and equilibrium in the early 19th century. The men of the Enlightenment developed a psychology, a theory of human nature, but not a sociology. Sociology inevitably focuses upon the importance of groups and of group life; this the Enlightenment theorists were not willing to do. But when the sociology of change did emerge, in the mid-19th century period of bourgeois consolidation, its links with the Enlightenment were sufficient to distinguish it immediately from its predecessor, the sociology of conservation. It combined some similar themes, and some new ones: progress, evolution, realism, historical materialism, inevitability and determinism—the ideological noise of the later 19th century. The ideals, the values of the sociology of change were those of the Enlightenment; the same slogans used to carry out the bourgeois revolutions in France, England and the United States were extended to include the lower social and economic orders in Marxism.

The confusion of the concept of natural law characteristic of the sociology of change may be observed in the two major forms of that sociology, Marxist sociology and a liberal American sociology flourishing in the period between the two World Wars—particularly the Chicago school, emphasizing social process. The emphasis, as with the Enlightenment theorists, was on changing the real world so that it would conform to the ideal. But where, for the Enlightenment thinkers, groups were important only insofar as the application of reason freed the individual from their tyranny, the sociology of change benefited from the intervening development of the sociology of conservation, which provided it with some basic insights as to the nature of society and the character of group life. In Marxism (the best example of the sociology of change) the battle cries of liberty, equality and fraternity were combined with a striking sociological emphasis previously stressed by the European conservatives. This was the insight of the sociology of conservation, borrowed from the ideal of feudal order, which seemed so appealing to many thinkers after the terrors of the Revolution. To avoid the anarchic destruction of institutional ties which took place under liberalism and capitalism, the emphasis on the necessity of social bonds was absorbed into Marxism and became extremely important in later interpretations of Marx. This conservative idea was combined with the ideals of the Enlightenment in a dynamic secular faith. The natural laws of social life, discoverable by sociological science, were to be used to create the new, rationally-planned order. The old order had to be transformed by the exercise of sociological knowledge in the service of revolutionary power.

This conception of natural laws, in slightly altered form, may be observed in another variant of the sociology of change: liberal American sociology dedicated to social engineering on behalf of liberal goals. As a form of the confusion of the natural law concept, this is less important because of the degree of methodological awareness among 20th century American sociologists.[12] However, insofar as it was actually liberal, this aspect of American sociology is a genuine sociology of change; it was and to some extent still is dedicated to the emancipation of the individual from traditional group tyrannies: ethnic and racial discrimination, the provincialism of the American small town, and for some, the autocracy of a factory system dominated by family capitalism. However, as I have indicated before, the idea of a liberal-individualist sociology is somewhat contradictory. The individualist who at the same time insists that the individual is not to be disconnected from the groups in which he participates—in fact, that he is to be understood as a resultant of group forces, a mere product of group affiliations[13]—cannot escape a feeling of self-contradiction. It becomes rather difficult to preserve some kind of autonomy for the individual and for the concept of individuality.

This inconsistent liberal-individualist sociology is a sociology of change, as is a collectivist version like Marxism. The sociology of change emphasizes the aim of prediction and control for sociological science, whether to implement liberal-individualist or collectivist goals. The natural laws it wishes to discover are not inevitable and inflexible workings out of an

---

[12] Here I have in mind the work of such men as Louis Wirth, Robert M. MacIver, Arnold Rose, Robert K. Merton, Herbert Hyman and Edward Shils.

[13] The psychologists' conception of personality is quite different. This is very far from being a dead issue among social scientists and is now the subject of an uneasy truce between sociologists and psychologists, with social psychologists ranged on both sides of the question. For an example of how this affects conceptualization and research see Jessie Bernard, "The Sociological Study of Conflict," *The Nature of Conflict* (Paris: UNESCO, 1957), p. 51.

inscrutable World Spirit, as is often the case in the sociology of conservation in the 19th century. Instead, these laws are viewed as potentially useful to men interested in intervention in the course of history—in social engineering.[14] Unlike the sociology of conservation of the early 19th century, however, a given state of affairs is not justified and rendered inevitable in terms of the working out of the laws of nature; rather, the discovery of those laws permits the engineering of the environment in accordance with specific ideals, which are themselves justified as being "natural" laws or rights.

For the sociology of conservation, on the other hand, the laws of social life operate as inevitable limitations on any foolish utopianism of a liberal-individualistic or collectivistic variety (depending on which kind of order is being defended). In the mind of the sociologist of conservation, the inevitability of these laws is of a piece with their intrinsic justice and goodness. The natural order of things must not be disturbed, and woe to the meddler who does not heed the warnings of sociological science, for he will only end by making more trouble than would have resulted if things had only been let alone. The sociologist of conservation must point out the absurdity, to paraphrase Sumner, of trying to make the world over, in order to save us from the inevitable disasters attending intervention in the natural processes of life.[15]

[14] It is true that some 20th century sociologists of conservation are interested in social engineering, but their sociology is formulated in terms of the preservation of social order. The sociology of Talcott Parsons is an example; cf. Alvin W. Gouldner, "Some Observations on Systematic Theory," *Sociology in the U.S.A.* (Paris: UNESCO, 1956) pp. 34-42; David Lockwood, "Some Remarks on 'The Social System,' " *British Journal of Sociology*, Vol. 7, No. 2, June, 1956; and Moore, *op. cit.*, p. 111 and *passim*.

[15] Sumner declares: "Sociology is the science of life in society . . . Its practical utility consists in deriving the rules of right social living from the facts and laws [*sic*] which prevail by nature in the constitution and functions of society . . . To err in prescribing for a man is at worst to kill him; to err in prescribing for a society is to set in operation injurious forces which extend, ramify, and multiply their effects in ever new combinations throughout an indefinite future." "Sociology," *Collected Essays in Political and Social Science*, reprinted in Perry Miller (ed.), *American Thought*. (New York: Rinehart, 1954), pp. 72, 75.

"History has but one cry, to teach us that the revolutions begun by the wisest men are always ended by the foolish; that the authors of them are always victims, and that the efforts of peoples to create or increase their liberty almost always end by giving them chains. An abyss is to be seen on every side."[16]

From this standpoint Sumner and de Maistre are intellectual cousins. Both are sociologists of conservation, although the orders each defend are quite different. De Maistre looks back nostalgically at the social aspects of the Middle Ages and dreams of potential ultramontane power amid the pageantry of the *ancien régime*. Sumner tries to defend the supremacy of the middle class with Spencerian formulas of *laissez-faire* individualism. The order of Sumner is that associated with the Adam Smith of the economics textbooks—the harmonious interweaving of the activities of enlightened, self-interested men. The content of the two sociologies is as different as the form is similar.

By now the difficulties of these categories should be clear. I call Sumner, who was a liberal and an individualist, a sociologist of conservation, although I have said that American liberal-individualist sociology must be classified as a sociology of change. The deciding factor, I would say, would be Sumner's conception of sociology and its uses, of sociological laws, and the function of the sociologist. In his theory of the inevitability of the kind of order to which he was almost theologically committed, that of a bourgeois *laissez-faire* economy with its corresponding social forms, Sumner shows himself to

---

[16] Joseph de Maistre, "Du Pape," *op. cit.*, III, p. 171. Both de Maistre and Sumner are fond of biological analogies. Sumner utilizes Spencer's organic analogy, but de Maistre, no doubt wary about introducing an element of dynamism, favors references to plants. "We recognize in the plant a concealed power, a plastic force, an essential unity, which produces and conserves, which invariably tends toward its end, which appropriates what serves it and rejects what hinders it, which carries the sap needed to the utmost fibre of the utmost leaf, which combats, with all its forces, the diseases of the vegetable body. . . . Blind that we are! How can we believe that a political body does not also have its law, its spirit, its plastic force. . .?" *Etude, op. cit.*, p. 363, cited by Kramer, *loc. cit.*

be close to de Maistre, who had a similar conception of natural laws. Or to take another example, Marx is clearly a mixed case, since he stresses the concept of a new social order and even looks back upon the feudal order with something which might be similar to the nostalgia of the conservatives and reactionaries: "The bourgeoisie, wherever it has got the upper hand, has put an end to all feudal, patriarchial, idyllic relations. It has pitilessly torn asunder the motley feudal ties that bound man to his 'natural superiors' and has left remaining no other nexus between man and man than naked self-interest, than callous 'cash payment.' "[17]

Yet, because of his conception of the *uses* of sociology and his version of the "natural law" formulation, I have called him a sociologist of change. He is inconsistently interventionist in his conception of the uses of sociological inquiry. The legacy of Hegel leads him to stress the inevitability of the revolution and the eventual victory of the proletariat, but in his inconsistent emphasis on the role of the Communist vanguard in hastening the cataclysm, and in his stress on historical dynamics and the potentialities for change inherent in any historical situation, he cannot be regarded as a sociologist of conservation. He is concerned with social and economic processes, not with the preservation of an ideal state of equilibrium. In any event, it should be clear that in suggesting these categories I have indulged in some oversimplification, in the hope of discerning a pattern in certain movements of thought and suggesting certain fugitive theoretical relationships. I believe that these relationships are not without significance for contemporary sociology. A frame of reference, a concept, a research tradition, the presuppositions of a science—all may exert an important controlling influence on the results. The distinction between a sociology of conservation and a sociology of change may be heuristically justifiable, and my purpose here is to bring into relief the different traditions within which dis-

[17] Karl Marx and Friedrich Engels, *Manifesto of the Communist Party* (Chicago: Charles H. Kerr, 1940), p. 15.

cussion of the concept of mass society has taken place. It is possible that this discussion, although nominally carried on under the aegis of science, has been influenced by certain considerations which are not, strictly speaking, scientific. At the center of sociology stands the ideal of social order;[18] it gains expression in the characteristic concepts and problems of that field of inquiry. Although the concept of order is central, there are those who wish to preserve a given social order, and others who want to change it. But the politics of the sociology of conservation and the sociology of change will always be a politics of order, not of anarchy. The preoccupation with social disintegration is continuous up to the present day, and culminates in the European theory of mass society.

[18] See the instructive lament of an angry "collectivist" berating American sociologists: "But perhaps the science of society has something subversive about it even when it is pursued under conditions of political freedom. Is it not collectivist by nature? It is difficult to envisage an individualist sociology—a fact that may account for the curious unwillingness of individualist writers to tackle sociological problems properly so-called. If society were an assemblage of middle-class people with 'status' worries to keep them busy when they are not occupied with the more important business of earning money, a liberal sociology would doubtless in due course make its appearance. Indeed, it has done so—in the U.S. But precisely for this reason it is not concerned with those social problems [*sic*] that have become our daily preoccupation.

"It is difficult to escape the impression that sociology and collectivism are inherently related to each other." G. L. Arnold, "Collectivism Reconsidered," *British Journal of Sociology*, Vol. 6, No. 1, March 1955, p. 3.

CHAPTER TWO

EUROPEAN THEORIES OF THE MASS AND MASS SOCIETY

THE concept of the mass has an interesting history in the modern period. Although references to "the many" go back as far as the Platonic critique of democracy, the widespread use of the terms "mass" and "masses" has its origin in the ideological struggles of political and economic groups in Europe prior to the French Revolution. It is only after the Revolution, however, that the concept emerges as part of the political rhetoric of the early 19th century. Professor Hardman, in his sardonic article,[1] declares it to be "an elastic epithet devoid of any precise scientific content," and says that it "is more likely to reveal the point of view of the person using it than to clarify the phenomena in question."

". . . the older metaphorical connotations persist. Among unrepentant aristocrats, intellectual as well as political and social, the term is interchangeable with hoi polloi, rabble, canaille, the great unwashed; prefaced by a patronizing adjective it may become the 'suffering masses' of the humanitarian or the 'eager masses' of the educator; to the political leader it denotes those whose approval and backing he needs only at election time and to the colonially minded western European it is most apt to suggest the denizens of unindustrialized, that is, unenlightened, areas east of Suez and south of the equator—or beyond the Vistula. Based chiefly on external criteria, it is an essentially abstract concept and takes on color only when set against the articulate, politically or economically organized minority operating in a particular institutional context."[2]

[1] See J. B. S. Hardman, "Masses," *Encyclopedia of the Social Sciences*, pp. 197-201.

[2] *Ibid.*, p. 197. Writing from a socialist standpoint, Professor Hardman takes an extremely dim view of the concept of the mass expressed in theories of the *Volksgeist*. This conception of "masses" as a spiritual whole emphasizing national unity is regarded as potentially explosive and dangerous to

One of the reasons for the great variety of concepts of the mass is the fact that the term "mass" has been identified with the rhetoric of different political groups, changing with the historical context of post-Revolutionary Europe as the franchise and other rights and powers were extended to an expanding circle of the citizenry. Thus what had been part of the anti-bourgeois, aristocratic rhetoric following the French Revolution became something quite different following the victory of the *bourgeoisie*. With the spread of industrialism and the factory system, "the masses" are increasingly identified as the urban-industrial workers and discontented lower orders by the new middle-class rhetoric, whereas before it had been a term applied pejoratively to the *bourgeoisie* by defenders of the *ancien régime*.

With Marx, however, the word "masses" came to apply to that stratum of society engaged in industrial production but excluded from the ownership or control of the instruments of production—i.e., the proletariat.[3] (Marx did recognize divisions within the mass, such as the "industrial reserve army" and the "sphere of pauperism" [*Lumpenproletariat*].) Little did he realize that he would be followed by a "reserve army" of interpreters and popularizers who would establish the common usage of the term in political theory and propaganda, to the extent that it would even be taken up by his fiercest opponents.[4] And while, in the writings of Bakunin[5] and Sorel,[6]

---

the cause of socialist internationalism. More interesting, however, is the fact that Durkheim's concept of "social solidarity" is also indicted, on somewhat the same grounds. Emphasis on social solidarity by sociologists, since it stresses the bases of unity in society as a whole, is just as likely, in Hardman's view, to gloss over the hard realities of class conflict within that society. Thus Durkheim's sociology, with its stress on order, association and consensus, is condemned by a man of the Left as bourgeois. Such are the hazards of the dialectic.

[3] See Marx's interesting comments on Hegel's concept of the mass by contrast with his own, in T. B. Bottomore and M. Rubel (ed.), *Karl Marx: Selected Writings in Sociology and Social Philosophy* (London: Watts, 1956), p. 57; and also *ibid.*, pp. 140, 145.

[4] See William Graham Sumner, *Folkways* (Boston: Ginn & Co., 1906), pp. 45-47, 52-53. Sumner used the term but defined it differently as the

the idea became identified with a cult of blind power eventually taking form in a spontaneous uprising, the Soviets and Chinese Communists stretched its meaning to include the agrarian lower classes and peasants as well as the industrial proletariat.[7] In sociology the state of usage is reflected in the declaration of Professor Wilhelm Vleugels in his attempt to assess the concept: "Not only do different authors associate different concepts with the word 'mass': often the *same* author will use the word to designate different concepts."[8]

Another important aspect of the evolution of the concept in political theory is the shift of attitude which takes place among many liberals in the course of the 19th century. Although the ideals of the Enlightenment are retained, in many cases disillusionment with the liberal program is reflected in the extent to which "the masses," with their demands for social, cultural and political equality, are identified as a threat to a stable bourgeois social order. The fear of the majority expressed in the writings of de Tocqueville and John Stuart Mill represents a retreat from the happy confidence of Condorcet and Bentham.[9] Late 19th century liberalism as repre-

---

large group in society which supports the mores—similar to Bagehot's "bald man at the back of the omnibus."

[5] Mikhail Bakunin, *The Political Philosophy of Bakunin* (Glencoe: Free Press, 1953).

[6] Georges Sorel, *Reflections on Violence* (Glencoe: Free Press, 1950).

[7] See in this connection, David Mitrany, *Marx Against the Peasant* (Chapel Hill: University of North Carolina Press, 1951).

[8] Wilhelm Vleugels, "Der Begriff der Masse: Ein Beitrag zur Entwicklungsgeschichte der Massentheorie," *Jahrbuch fur Soziologie* II (Karlsruhe: Verlag G. Braun, 1926), p. 177. In the German literature the term means "crowd" more often than "mass." For a recent catalogue of usages, see also Paul Reiwald, *Vom Geist der Massen: Handbuch der Massenpsychologie* (Zurich: Pan-Verlag, 1948).

[9] See the excellent discussion of this point in Judith Shklar, *After Utopia* (Princeton: Princeton University Press, 1957), pp. 226-235.

Mill's fear of the majority found expression in statements which resemble those of the theorists of mass society: "At present individuals are lost in the crowd. In politics it is almost a triviality to say that public opinion now rules the world. The only power deserving the name is that of masses and of governments while they make themselves the organ of the tendencies and instincts [*sic*] of the masses. This is as true in the moral and social relations of private life as in public transactions. Those whose opinions go

sented by such thinkers as de Tocqueville, Mill, Acton and Burckhardt becomes a philosophy of retrenchment and nostalgia, with concomitant fear of and disillusion with the masses. This presents, to the intellectual historian at least, a paradoxical situation in which liberal thinkers evolve into theorists of mass society. But it is not sufficient to attempt to throw light on the origins of the theory of mass society in a purely political context, as its links with 19th century romanticism are perhaps even more important.

Broadly speaking, romanticism led in two principal directions: a celebration of the free individual on the one hand, and of the organic local, national or folk community on the other. That the idealization of the organic folk community was a significant theme in the intellectual history of the first half of the 19th century, and that it was important in connection with the rise of sociology itself, I have already indicated in Chapter One. The individualistic strand of romanticism underwent a transformation, however: the exultant Promethean loneliness of the Byronic hero was transformed in later 19th century sociology into the universal loneliness of the average man—the unheroic man in the mass. Sociological romanticism recombined the two strands of 19th century romanticism, on the one hand, in its idealization of the *Gemeinschaft*, and on the other, in its emphasis on the isolated, unhappy and alienated[10] individual, liberated from the traditional society and thrust into the impersonal and abstract

---

by the name of public opinion are not always the same sort of public: in America they are the whole white population; in England, chiefly the middle class. But they are always a mass, that is to say, a collective mediocrity." J. S. Mill, "On Liberty," *Utilitarianism, Liberty and Representative Government* (New York: Dutton, 1951), pp. 165-166.

[10] One of the most important sources of this critique is to be found in the writings of Schiller. See, for example, *The Aesthetic Letters, Essays and the Philosophical Letters of Schiller* (Boston: Little, Brown, 1845), fifth and sixth letters. Schiller's significance for later social theory is cited by F. Neumann, "Anxiety and Politics," *The Democratic and the Authoritarian State* (Glencoe: Free Press, 1957), p. 271: "What Schiller describes so impressively is what Hegel and Marx were to characterize as alienation."

world of "the city." The latter theme, so familiar to modern sociologists, was elaborated in some form or other in virtually every sociological theory of the later 19th and early 20th centuries. And some basic concepts that appeared in the sociology of the early 19th century—in French conservatism—were continually repeated themes in the French, German and English sociologies of the later 19th century, finally emerging in the European theory of mass society. Indeed, the theory of mass society seems to have developed out of 19th century sociology in a direct line of continuity. These two theories share a preoccupation with "social disorganization" and "social disintegration." The idea of the breakdown of the primary group in modern society was a fundamental theme of 19th century sociology, as it is for the theory of mass society. The emergence of a large-scale society, increasingly industrialized and concentrated in urban centers, became the focus of emphasis in the works of Ferdinand Tönnies,[11] Sir Henry Maine,[12] George Simmel,[13] Emile Durkheim[14] and Max Weber.[15] These theories resembled each other not only in their focus on the transition from a traditional to a rationalized society, but in their postulation of a necessary historical development—an evolutionary movement from the simple to the complex, the homogenous to the heterogenous, the undifferentiated to the differentiated.[16] They were all heavily

[11] F. Tönnies, *Fundamental Concepts of Sociology* (Gemeinschaft und Gesellschaft) trans. C. P. Loomis (New York: American Book Co., 1940). Tönnies acknowledges the influence of Sir Henry Maine in F. Tönnies, "Mein Verhältnis zur Soziologie," in R. Thurnwald (ed.), *Soziologie von Heute: Ein Symposium* (Leipzig: C. L. Hirschfeld, 1932).
[12] Sir Henry Maine, *Ancient Law* (London: J. M. Dent & Sons, 1917).
[13] G. Simmel (ed. K. H. Wolff), *The Sociology of Georg Simmel* (Glencoe: Free Press, 1950), Ch. 3-4.
[14] E. Durkheim, *The Division of Labor in Society*, ed. George Simpson (Glencoe: Free Press, 1949); *Suicide* (Glencoe: Free Press, 1951).
[15] Max Weber, *The Protestant Ethic and the Spirit of Capitalism* (London: George Allen & Unwin, 1930); *Essays on Sociology*, ed. H. H. Gerth and C. W. Mills (New York: Oxford University Press, 1946), especially Parts II, VII, and Parts IV, XIV.
[16] See Kenneth E. Bock, "The Acceptance of Histories: Toward a Perspective for Social Science," *University of California Publications in Sociol-*

influenced by the philosophy of history. The permissive sociological method of typology, the creation of "ideal types,"
allowed them to set up a series of dichotomies which in each
case reflected the distinction between the transition from status
to contract (Maine), community to society (Tönnies), mechanical to organic solidarity (Durkheim) and traditional to
legal-rational authority (Weber).

This perspective of 19th century sociology is recapitulated
in the 20th century theory of mass society, particularly in its
view of the past. By contrast with the anarchic individualism
of life in the cities, the impersonality of social relationships,
the peculiar mental qualities fostered by urban life with its
emphasis on money and abstraction, theorists of mass society
idealized the social aspects of the traditional society of the
later middle ages. They stressed the importance of the small
or "primary" group: the family, the small occupational groups
and guilds, the church group, the communal circle—all characterized by face-to-face relationships and strong mutual identification enhanced by the small size of the groups and the
physical proximity of the members. Even Marx shared this
view of "feudal, idyllic relations," as we have seen; and many
of the same ideas could be found in the literature of guild
socialism,[17] a sure indication that these ideas were not the
exclusive property of the Right. As advanced by sociologists
in its 20th century form, the theory of mass society combines
these elements in a formulation which often involves "a presumed scientific statement concerning the disorganization of
society created by industrialization and by the demand of the
masses for equality."[18]

---

ogy, Vol. 3, No. 1, 1956. The author suggests that the idea of a "development" here is an assumption and not a hypothesis which could be verified
empirically. As such, it is based on the illegitimate use of biological analogies, the conceptual identification of social process with organic growth
process. See *ibid.*, pp. 114-115.

[17] See A. J. Penty, *The Restoration of the Gild System* (London: S.
Sonenschein, 1906). Cited by Bell, *infra*.

[18] Daniel Bell, "The Theory of Mass Society," *Commentary*, July 1956,
p. 77. I am indebted to Professor Bell for providing the stimulus for the

"Behind the theory of social disorganization lies a romantic notion of the past that sees society as having once been made up of small 'organic,' close-knit communities that were shattered by industrialism and modern life, and replaced by a large impersonal 'atomistic' society which is unable to provide the basic gratifications and call forth the loyalties that the older communities knew."[19]

Professor Bell has attempted to summarize the main points of the theory of mass society, which he declares to be "central to the thinking of the principal aristocratic, Catholic, or Existentialist critics of bourgeois society today."

"The revolutions in transport and communications have brought men into closer contact with each other and bound them in new ways; the division of labor has made them more interdependent; tremors in one part of society affect all others. Despite this greater interdependence, however, individuals have grown more estranged from one another. The old primary group ties of family and local community have been shattered; ancient parochial faiths are questioned; few unifying values have taken their place. Most important, the critical standards of an educated elite no longer shape opinion or taste. As a result, mores and morals are in constant flux, relations between individuals are tangential or compartmentalized rather than organic. At the same time greater mobility, spatial and social, intensifies concern over status. Instead of a fixed or known status symbolized by dress or title, each person assumes a multiplicity of roles and constantly has to prove himself in a succession of new situations. Because of all this, the individual loses a coherent sense of self. His anxieties increase. There ensues a search for new faiths. The stage is thus set for the charismatic leader, the secular messiah, who, by bestowing upon each person the semblance of necessary

---

effort to isolate the common elements in the theory of mass society among thinkers of varying political faiths. His article represents the most perceptive treatment of the entire problem.

[19] *Ibid.*

grace, and of fullness of personality, supplies a substitute for the older unifying belief that the mass society has destroyed."[20]

As here represented, the theory of mass society suggests a crystallization and convergence of the major themes of 19th century sociology. This helps us to understand the curious circumstances under which thinkers of both Right and Left are united in agreement on the fundamentals of the mass society theory. Both sociologists of conservation and sociologists of change hold these ideas in common. The emphasis on order which is fundamental to sociology is brought to a focus in the theory of mass society. The villain of the piece is individualist-liberalism in both instances, although the "scientific" character of the theory of mass society is not stressed by thinkers of the Right, or by its Christian Existentialist exponents.[21]

We are more interested in those thinkers, however, who claim that their theory of the mass society is scientific, and rather less in those who, philosophically opposed to liberalism, industrialism and secularism, attack them as the causes of all our present ills, conveniently embodied in the idea of mass society. The scientific conception of mass society is extremely influential. It forms part of the intellectual equipment of social scientists and others in all parts of Europe, and has gained many converts in the United States. Its main themes may be discerned in a wide range of the most influential books in economics, sociology and political science.[22]

[20] *Ibid.*, p. 75.

[21] See, for example, Gabriel Marcel, *Men Against Humanity* (London: Harvill Press, 1952); Karl Jaspers, *Man in the Modern Age* (London: Routledge, Kegan Paul, 1951), and *The Origin and Goal of History* (London: Routledge, Kegan Paul, 1953).

[22] For example, Karl Polanyi, *The Great Transformation* (Boston: Beacon Press, 1957), p. 33, *passim*. The self-regulating market mechanism is viewed as having ground "men into masses." Here economic and social planning are recommended as the antidote to the excesses of individualism under early capitalism.

In Erich Fromm's *Escape from Freedom* (London: Routledge, Kegan Paul, 1942), p. 39, the idea of a mass is presented in the following terms: those people who, in former times, constituted the lower orders of society, have lost their previous sense of status and security because of the rise of

How has this theory been applied in the effort to explain social and political phenomena? Serious students of modern political development, for example, have declared that totalitarianism is a result of the conditions of mass society. The sociologist Karl Mannheim has asserted that "the main changes we are witnessing today can ultimately be traced to the fact that we are living in a Mass Society."[23] Although she does not use the concept of "mass society," Hannah Arendt's analysis of the role of the masses in the rise of totalitarianism is quite characteristic of theorists of mass society: "The truth is that the masses grew out of the fragments of a highly atomized society whose competitive structure and concomitant loneliness of the individual had been held in check only through membership in a class. The chief characteristic of the mass man is not brutality and backwardness, but his isolation and lack of normal social relationships. Coming from the class-ridden society of the nation-state, whose cracks had been cemented with nationalist sentiment, it is only natural that these masses, in the first helplessness of their new experience, have tended toward an especially violent nationalism, to which mass leaders have yielded against their own instincts and purposes for purely demagogic reasons."[24]

It is difficult to see how Arendt's discussion of masses could possibly apply to Soviet Russia, in spite of her ingenious effort

---

industrialism and the resulting strains of urban life. In this bewildered state they are subject to anxiety and are easily manipulated and exploited by those in power, or by demagogues aspiring to power.

In Sebastian de Grazia, *The Political Community* (Chicago: University of Chicago Press, 1952), the dominant concept is that of Durkheimian *anomie*; the solution to "social pathology" is suggested in submission to a wider, all-embracing body such as the Roman Church which would provide agreement on fundamentals and a salutary consensus. See also John A. Hallowell, *The Decline of Liberalism as an Ideology* (London: Routledge, Kegan Paul, 1946), for a similar line of thought in political theory.

[23] Karl Mannheim, *Diagnosis of Our Time* (London: Routledge, Kegan Paul, 1943), p. 1.

[24] H. Arendt, *Origins of Totalitarianism* (New York: Harcourt, 1951), pp. 310-311. Criticism of Arendt's work is offered here without any intention of minimizing her extraordinary contribution to the understanding of modern history.

to show that Stalin had to create an artificially "atomized" situation before totalitarian rule was possible, a situation which she says history had already created in Germany for Hitler at the time he seized power. Phrases like "highly atomized society," "competitive structure" and "loneliness of the individual," although they have good standing in that aspect of the theory of mass society which combines Marxism and German sociological romanticism, hardly seem adequate in describing the Russia of 1917 or even the China of 1949.

That mass society is the result of the rise of liberalism and the social and cultural by-product of the process of urbanization and industrialization is itself an exceedingly ambiguous notion. Those who hold that mass society causes totalitarianism must deal with the obvious fact that totalitarianism came to Russia, a backward and relatively underdeveloped nation, as well as to urbanized and industrialized Germany, and that it has not made its appearance in other such urbanized and industrialized nations as England and the United States. Arendt is simplifying the issue in somewhat the same way that Marx did himself: she is ignoring existing divisions and loyalties within the classes and across them, of a local, regional and national character.[25]

[25] There is today a radical movement which tends to sweep over and ignore local, regional and even national differences, but it is not the organized proletarian movement of the industrialized countries which Marx predicted. "It is rather an international protest movement against the countries of western civilization in which industrialization has bestowed major benefits on the working masses. All countries outside this civilization continue to struggle with the problem of transforming their peasant masses into an industrial work-force. The masses themselves are caught in the dilemma of not being able to survive either in cities that are not industrialized enough to absorb them or in villages that are too overcrowded and poor to yield them a subsistence. Confronted, in addition, with a steadily increasing availability of diverse commodities which they cannot buy, they experience an intensification of the poverty which they cannot escape. For these reasons, peasant uprisings, the organization of hitherto inert masses under communist leadership, and the effective transformation of discontent into a militant nationalist movement are likely to occur in the countries of comparative disadvantage with regard to industrialization. The ruling groups within each of these underdeveloped areas will strain every effort in order to transform a discontent which is often directed against them

The philosophical premises from which such analyses as that of Arendt are rationalistically derived are crucial for the theory of mass society. Among such theorists the concept of "the mass" often involves a corresponding concept of "the elite." One of the elements which unites the theorists of mass society is their elitism. The elite concept emerges in conjunction with their preference for a *Standesgesellschaft*, a hierarchically organized social order, the ideal for which is often sought in medieval models or in an extremely rationalized version of the modern division of labor. The rise of the masses signals the breakdown of the distinctions between the different ranks of society and results in cultural and political decline and degeneration. The levelling process in the cultural sphere has a political source. Thus Ortega y Gasset, writing within a literary and philosophical tradition rather than under the aegis of science, proclaims a doctrine of the disintegration of the elites which evokes echoes from other theorists of mass society,[26] notably in the work of Mannheim. The egalitarian side of liberalism threatens even those heavily influenced by the Marxist tradition, for the elitism which lay suppressed and undeveloped in Marx's own writings, in his neglect of the bureaucratic development necessary to carry through the revolution, was developed later by Lenin and others to the extent that the elitism of the Marxist intellectuals became a marked aspect of their social theories—as for example in the work of Mannheim. Thus in the view of Arendt, the spread of general education results in an "inevitable lowering of standards and popularizing of content."[27] The rise of mass

---

into a unified nationalist movement which is directed instead against the 'imperialists' of the West. Hence, the major determinants of the struggle for power in these areas cannot be ascertained by an analysis of their social stratification, but rather by emphasizing that class differences have come to be subordinated to the much more decisive conflict between the underdeveloped areas and the industrialized West." Reinhard Bendix, "Social Stratification and Political Power," *Class Status and Power* (Glencoe: Free Press, 1953), p. 598.

[26] See *infra*, Chapter Six.

[27] A confirmation of this interpretation was provided unexpectedly by

culture, an inevitable concomitant of the theory of mass society, will be discussed in Chapter Six.

Ortega y Gasset's views are those of a Spanish liberal influenced by German romanticism. In previous times, according to Ortega, men lived on the land, in the villages or in the towns, and each occupied a specific place and a specific status. These people are now displaced, and this displacement converts them into masses. But the idea of the mass has other meanings; society is always made up of two components: creative, select minorities, and masses. The difference between these is that the former are "specially qualified," the latter "essentially unqualified." The basis for the distinction, however, appears to be that the select man is the one who drives himself on to higher goals, a Faustian perfectionist who is never satisfied with himself as he *is*: "For there is no doubt that the most radical division that it is possible to make of humanity is that which splits it into two classes of creatures: those who make great demands on themselves, piling up difficulties and duties; and those who demand nothing special of themselves, but for whom to live is to be every moment what they already are, without imposing on themselves any effort toward perfection. . . ."[28]

This division into mass and select minorities is not to be interpreted as reflecting the division into social classes. Ortega declares that select men may be found also in the lower classes, although the chances of their being found in the upper classes are rather greater: "It is, of course, plain that in these 'upper' classes, when and as long as they really are so, there is much

---

Dr. Arendt herself in "Reflections on Little Rock," *Dissent*, Winter 1959. There she argues against government intervention to safeguard civil rights and against desegregation in education. She declares that discrimination in the social sphere is legitimate, and that the achievement of equality by Negroes in the U. S. would exacerbate the color problem instead of relieving it. She demonstrates here the prejudice of many theorists of mass society against equality of opportunity and social mobility in favor of a more stable society.

[28] José Ortega y Gasset, *The Revolt of the Masses* (New York: Pelican, 1950), p. 10.

more likelihood of finding men who adopt the 'great vehicle,' whereas the 'lower' classes normally comprise individuals of minus quality."[29]

Here, as elsewhere, Ortega is involved in self-contradiction and systematic ambiguity. In previous times, he says, the mass had no desire to intervene in these special functions of a cultural and political character which are properly the concern of the select minorities. "They recognized their place in a healthy dynamic [*sic*] social system." The new attitude on the part of the masses, which is implied in the title of Ortega's book, is that they are no longer content with this state of affairs. The masses have invaded the places never intended for them, and are progressively supplanting the creative minorities. The inevitable results of this process are the disintegration of culture and the total corruption of political life.

The archetype of the mass man for Ortega, however, is the specialist, the technician, the scientist. This is due to the character of science itself, which is concerned with *minutiae* and encourages ignorance of the rest of the universe of culture.[30] This does serve to set Ortega apart from some other theorists of mass society who are by no means so unfavorably disposed toward "science," and in fact consider their own work to be scientific.[31] Here as elsewhere it should be clear that Ortega is using words dialectically and that "the masses" or the "mass-man" is used as a rhetorical device to lend a pejorative connotation to those elements of modern culture and politics which he finds distasteful.[32]

[29] *Ibid.*, p. 10.
[30] *Ibid.*, pp. 79-81.
[31] Ortega contradicts himself here as well; he is not above using the results of demography to press a point, as in his cry concerning the increase of population in Europe. "The fact is this: from the time European history begins in the sixth century up to the year 1800—that is, through the course of twelve centuries—Europe does not succeed in reaching a total population greater than 180 million inhabitants. Now from 1800 to 1914—little more than a century—the population of Europe mounts from 180 millions to 460 millions!" *Ibid.*, p. 35.
[32] Ortega has influenced the Christian existentialists in this respect, with

With Mannheim the issue is joined in a somewhat different way. Although he and Ortega share in Hegel a common intellectual ancestor, part of Mannheim's thought is the result of a line of development frequently identified as "Left-Hegelian"—best represented by Marx—while Ortega's can be considered at least in part as an offshoot of the "Right-Hegelian" wing. The work of Mannheim is well known in the United States as well as in Western Europe. He develops a theory of "mass society" along the lines already indicated, perhaps emphasizing the socio-psychological aspects rather than the more purely sociological forces at work, and stressing the inadequacy of traditional liberalism to cope with the situation. His elite theory, however, does not reach its fullest expression until his residence in England. The masses are viewed as the culturally and politically unsophisticated majority who succeed in infiltrating the culture-bearing elites. The breakdown of these elites is the result of the "fundamental democratization" and levelling of culture in the liberal democracies; and the fascist and communist dictatorships represent attempts at social reconstruction in the effort to deal with this problem.

"The crisis of culture in liberal-democratic society is due, in the first place, to the fact that the social processes, which previously favored the development of the creative elites, now have the opposite effect, i.e., have become obstacles to the forming of elites because wider sections of the population still under unfavourable social conditions take an active part in cultural activities."[33]

In liberal society, according to Mannheim, the number of elite groups increases progressively, resulting in a diminution

---

his concepts of the "mass-man" and "mass society." See the acknowledgment of indebtedness in Karl Jaspers, *The Origin and Goal of History* (London: Routledge, 1953), p. 281; and in Gabriel Marcel, *Men Against Humanity* (London: Harvill Press, 1952), pp. 103-104.

[33] Karl Mannheim, *Man and Society in an Age of Reconstruction* (New York: Harcourt Brace, 1950), p. 85.

of their power. The exclusiveness of these groups is destroyed, thereby removing the social context which, in his view and also that of T. S. Eliot,[34] is essential for the survival of culture. There follows a change in the principle of selection of these elites, in which objective criteria of achievement are sacrificed to the notion of "equalizing opportunities." This results in the degeneration of liberal mass society into fascism. Finally, the composition of the elite changes and results in the leadership of the "essentially unqualified." This entire discussion in Mannheim is marked by a free transfer of concepts from psychology into the sociological sphere, and abounds with psychological analogies which are suggestive but quite confusing. But apart from the scientific explanation of these events, it is clear that Mannheim views the *Standesgesellschaft* as not only inevitable but also desirable: without it the culture-bearing elites do not survive. All "social reconstruction" has ultimate reference to it as an ideal; the classless society may be one in which culture has ceased to exist.

This is also the burden of Lederer's book, an interesting and unusual document completed shortly before the author's death. Lederer had been an eminent Marxist economist and social theorist; his book represents a personal revolt against the Marxist framework. For him the mass society is the Marxist ideal of the classless one. Lederer is interested in exposing this concept as a threat to civilization: "It is the theme of this book to show that society is always stratified, and that not only its productivity but also its cultural evolution depends upon an independent group life."[35]

[34] The agreement on fundamentals of the man of the Left and the man of the Right is striking, and should provide a clue as to the misleading character of these labels, which in this case conceal more than they reveal. Thus Mr. Eliot acknowledges his considerable debt to Professor Mannheim in the preface to his *Notes Toward a Definition of Culture* and declares: "I attempt, as far as possible, to contemplate my problems from the point of view of the sociologist and not from that of the Christian apologist. . . . It is an essential condition of the preservation of the quality of the culture of the minority, that it should continue to be a minority culture" (pp. 68, 107).

[35] Emil Lederer, *The State of the Masses* (New York: Norton, 1940),

But Lederer's revolt against the Marxist framework is a partial failure, because he is trapped in the dialectic itself. He is incapable of visualizing social stratification and social organization different from the Marxist conception of classes. All institutional life is forced into the class mold. From the antithesis of masses and classes there is no escape. Thus he reasons that since the ideal of the classless society is incorrect, the alternative is the traditional class structure, the *status quo*.

"The real opposites are states based on stratified society and states based on masses. The state of the older type, based on a stratified society, might be progressive or reactionary: history was molded by these states up to the emergence of the state of the masses. The state of the masses can probably be equally progressive or reactionary, though the distinction would lose much of its weight."[36]

As the above paragraph indicates, the author's attitude toward the Soviet Union is hopelessly ambiguous.

"It is still uncertain whether and when this dictatorial regime based on force can be transformed into a free society with free opinion and free discussion, where life again becomes productive and spontaneous. Such a concentrated system is probably not at all conducive to a loose structure with ample leeway for individuals and groups."[37]

Lederer's preference for the *Standesgesellschaft* is dramatized in his discussion of masses and classes. Crowds and masses are identified with the emotions, and with the "lower" self. Reason is identified with the existence of classes, true society, and the "higher" self. In this recapitulation of the

---

p. 206. Similarities of the main lines of thought in these and other theorists of mass society is striking. See the comments of Judith Shklar, *After Utopia* (Princeton: Princeton University Press, 1958), pp. 160-161, where the author emphasizes the similarities of the analyses of Arendt and Lederer; she stresses the relation to romanticism of their concepts of the masses and the influence of Le Bon and the irrationalists, which she claims followed upon the authors' disillusionment with Marx.

[36] *Ibid.*, p. 66.
[37] *Ibid.*, p. 208.

language of Burke, the link between the early 19th century conservatives and the Marxists is clearly revealed: both are critics of liberalism, of individualism; both are exponents of the hierarchically-arranged society, although they champion different strata. Burke's praise of habit and custom would make no sense to Lederer the rationalist, yet the latter had come full-circle, in defending the idea of a structured social order as based on "reason." It is ironic that Lederer should have viewed his preference for the *Standesgesellschaft* as a revolt against the Marxian conception of a classless society. There is a double irony in that the principle of order and hierarchy had already been firmly incorporated in the structure of Soviet society at the time of his writing, and yet he still entertained the hope that the future might bring a realization of the Marxist ideal in that country.

It has already been suggested that thinkers of both Left and Right share a common view of the theory of mass society. One aspect of this common viewpoint has also been indicated: that the idea of the mass generates a complementary concept, the idea of the elite. The elitism of theorists of mass society, both Right and Left, indicates again that in part this theory rests not on empirical research alone, but on a specifically anti-liberal philosophical approach to modern society. It is derived from a number of assumptions concerning modern society, few of them proven or even provable by scientific methods.[38] Many of the propositions on which the theory of mass society is based are not of the type which can be declared true or false. That is, they do not involve questions of fact, but rather, questions of fact structured by and saturated with values. They resemble philosophical rather than scientific propositions. In the analysis of the mass society theorists, where such proposi-

---

[38] Professor Bell remarks that "out of these biases has come the image of masses and leadership in which description and value judgment have become so intertwined as to warp, for scientific purposes, a large number of social studies. See "Notes on Authoritarian and Democratic Leadership," *Studies in Leadership*, Alvin Gouldner (ed.), (New York: Harper, 1950), p. 399.

tions are presented as science, value judgments are being disguised as facts. This is not an act of conscious deception on the part of these theorists, but their key propositions are so loaded with intellectual freight in the form of value judgments that they cannot be considered "scientific" in the ordinary sense. This calls for an elaboration of the role of value judgments in social science conceptualization and research, to which I will return in the final chapter.

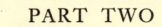

PART TWO

CHAPTER THREE

EUROPEANS AND AMERICANS ON THE CROWD:
THE CONCEPT OF COLLECTIVE BEHAVIOR

WE have said that one of the aims of this study is to employ a comparative approach in the analysis of similar American and European materials, with emphasis on the unique characteristics of each, rather than on their similarities. I will resist the impulse to charge at full gallop over an old battlefield—the question of whether the historian studies uniqueness and the sociologist studies similarities. This issue, much fought over in Germany during the late nineteenth century, has acquired a Teutonic air; but it is partially a semantic problem. Given the context of inquiry—a widely diffused lack of interest and understanding of the differences between the European and American approaches to the subject among the generally ahistorical practitioners of the sociological art in the United States—it will be more useful to stress the differences. A study of these differences will tell us a great deal about American sociology—a subject not much studied from an historical or a sociological standpoint by sociologists themselves.

The most interesting thing about American sociology in the twentieth century, in its relation to the European theories thus far discussed, is that in many instances where it has been influenced by a European tradition, one of two things have resulted. On the one hand, there has been either a transformation of the meanings of the European concepts, or the development of new concepts more appropriate to the American liberal tradition and the American social and political context; on the other, there has been an uncritical application of concepts developed in Europe to American data without regard for the resulting distortions or for the special conditions which had to be taken into account.

Both of these results may be seen in the treatment of the themes of "social disorganization," "social problems," "social pathology," "social control" and, more recently, "deviant behavior." In the lexicon of sociology these terms designate roughly similar areas of interest. To simplify somewhat, the difference between the American and the European treatments may be seen as the difference between the studies of "social problems" and "the social problem" respectively. The first indicates a field of research resulting in long, detailed studies of juvenile delinquency, alcoholism, divorce, criminality, race relations, minority problems, poverty and slums. It is a field of endeavor at least part of which might be summarized by saying that it represents an effort to make intransigent individuals and groups of different races, nationalities, ethnic origins, creeds, religions and economic statuses behave like white, Protestant, northern members of the American middle class. Agreement among many early twentieth-century American sociologists on the absolute validity of the middle-class norm is unanimous despite the fact that this notion is occasionally entertained unawares. And, as we approach mid-century, this unconscious assumption finds expression, and the adequacy of the middle-class norm is made explicit: "Now it is a difficult task to socialize in the middle class way of behavior those great masses of low-status children who form the bulk of the schools' population. Yet this is what American public education really attempts. We must learn, therefore, how to motivate low-status children and adults, bound by their own many-sided culture in the family, church and organizations, by means of socially adaptive forms of anxiety. In order, however, to make low-status children *anxious* to work hard, study hard, save more money, and accept stricter sex mores, our society must convince them of the *reality* of the *rewards* at the end of the anxiety-laden climb. To the upper-middle class child who learns well and climbs fast, the prestige rewards appear large, certain, and relatively near. Our society cannot hope, therefore, to educate the great masses of lower-class people in any really effective manner until it has *real* rewards to offer them for learning the necessary anxiety."[1]

But these areas of interest, these "social problems," are a far cry from being the same as "the social problem" of the European sociologists. The latter turns on the stubborn question of the relations among the social classes—a question historically and traditionally defined which, as Americans now realize to an increasing extent, is rather unrelated to the fact that one American drives a Ford while another drives a Cadillac. Some Europeans sociologists have understood this more readily than the Americans; thus Mannheim, who unfortunately did not write more than a few pages on this topic, after citing the dissatisfaction of Europeans with much of American sociological research because of its tendency to concentrate on isolated parts (delinquency, slums, divorce) without giving any consideration to the whole, declares: "On the other hand, there is another reason why our claims on social science are not satisfied by typical American contributions to this science, interesting and valuable as they may be in themselves. This reason is that typical American studies start from questions in no wise connected with those problems which arouse our passions in everyday political and social struggle."[2]

What better way of saying that America's unique social and political tradition, her liberalism, has somehow warped her sociology so that it is different from that which Europeans practice and comprehend? Those burning issues which aroused the passions of Europeans in social and political conflict are precisely the issues which have, to a large extent, ceased to be matters of controversy in the United States since the time of

---

[1] Allison Davis, "Socialization and Adolescent Personality," in Swanson, Newcomb and Hartley, *Readings in Social Psychology* (New York: Henry Holt and Co., 1952), p. 531. The middle-class bias of American sociologists is also illustrated in the preconceptions of the theory of social mobility: Professor Edward Tiryakian has pointed out to me that upward mobility is often viewed as the result of aspiration, while downward mobility is a result of circumstances.

[2] Karl Mannheim, *Essays on Sociology and Social Psychology* (London: Routledge, Kegan Paul, 1953), p. 191.

Jackson, if not from the beginning. It is no accident then (to echo the determinist rhetoric of Marxism) that sociology in America is a rather different proposition from sociology in Europe. A transplanted European sociologist has remarked that America is the only place where sociology is practiced without socialism.[3] But as everyone knows, European socialism has never been an important force in American politics. Professor Hartz has argued, I think cogently, that it was the absence of a prior feudal tradition in America which accounted for the failure of the appearance of a powerful socialist movement.[4] The language of order is presupposed in the socialist rhetoric, as I have tried to show in the previous chapters by tracing the links between the Left and the Right. But the fortunate Americans, beginning their national career with a tradition of liberalism, do not develop a sociology sensitized to "the social problem," for the same reason that they do not develop a vital socialism. Sociology, in fact, becomes something quite

[3] Albert Salomon, *The Tyranny of Progress* (New York: Noonday, 1955), p. 22.

[4] Louis Hartz, *The Liberal Tradition in America* (New York: Harcourt Brace, 1955). The extent of my indebtedness to Professor Hartz should be obvious. A recent commentator has described his thesis as follows: "Following de Tocqueville, Hartz sees the American as having been 'born free' in that he has never had to revolt against a domestic feudalism in order to arrive at liberal democracy. By comparison with Europe the United States was born a liberal country with limited government, social mobility and economic freedom. Without an aristocracy for an ally or a proletariat for an enemy the American middle-class has perpetually frustrated the growth of either a European-style conservatism or socialism, which require the seed-bed of feudal hierarchy. Liberals, having no *ancien régime* to attack, have been sober, moderate and realistic. American 'conservatism' in a non-feudal society has been the bourgeois gospel of work and success, reeking with liberal praise of mobility and competition, or an obscurantist Americanism which, in its nightmarish fears of a radical bogey, has hugged to its breast in a blind passion the fetishistic idol of a Constitution that is itself the product of a liberal ethos. What threatens American culture, in Hartz' judgment, is the universal implicit acceptance of a Lockeian vision of individuals with natural rights in an atomistic society where government is always the dread Leviathan. Culture-bound by the liberal realities of American life, liberalism becomes innocent and dogmatic, only half-conscious of itself for lack of an authentic, feudally-based conservatism with which to grapple." (Cushing Strout, "Liberalism, Conservatism and the Babel of Tongues," *Partisan Review*, Winter 1958, pp. 105-106.)

different in America, and this is the reason that it survives at all. Had sociology become *identified* with European socialism, it probably would have disappeared.

If we overlook the historicist flavor of this formulation, and look at the history of American sociology, there is evidence that sociology did become something quite different in the United States. It became identified with what Mannheim calls "social policy," and what I have called "social problems"; in the case of the immigrants this meant the subversion of many "old world traits transplanted," and in the case of rural migrants to the big cities meant gradual assimilation to a middle-class standard of life. Thus the difference between a sociology of conservation and a sociology of change is brought into sharp relief: the 20th century American sociologists of conservation were concerned with maintaining the American norm and assimilating vast numbers of "deviants" (both from within and without) to that norm; the European sociologists of change emphasized ultimate and irreducible conflicts of classes which would hasten the reorganization of the entire social system on a new economic and social basis.

Of course I am here discussing dominant trends, and realize full well that exceptions exist in both cases—not unusual in view of the exchange of viewpoints which became more frequent as the 19th century gave way to the 20th, as American sociologists went to Europe to sit at the feet of the great men in their field. Many of the leaders in American sociology at the turn of the century who had studied in Germany, subsequently founded the Chicago school which, for thirty years, was synonymous with sociology in America.[5] Albion Small, who founded the Department of Sociology at the University of Chicago in 1891, had studied at Leipzig and Berlin with Gustav Schmoller and Adolf Wagner; Robert E. Park studied at Berlin and Heidelberg with Georg Simmel and Wilhelm Windelband; W. I. Thomas had studied and travelled extensively in Europe (although he was far from

[5] See Albion Small, *Origins of Sociology* (Chicago: University of Chicago Press, 1924), pp. 325-326.

enthusiastic about German sociology), and was very much influenced by Florian Znaniecki in the course of their collaboration on *The Polish Peasant in Europe and America.* The development of sociology at Chicago represents a separate study which is somewhat outside the scope of this essay, but its relevance to the theory of mass society *and* as a comparative case study in the political context of sociological inquiry is undeniable. I will have reference later to the work of the Chicago sociologists relevant to the discussion of collective and mass behavior in the United States.

The exchange of viewpoints mentioned above became much more commonplace after the rise of totalitarianism sent hundreds of émigré scholars to American universities, where they entered directly into the intellectual life of the country. That some were dissatisfied with the American version of a European social science we have already seen.[6] Their presence in larger numbers and the quality of their work made for an increased awareness in the United States of the existence of real differences of opinion as to the proper approach to sociology.

Now these comments on the general character of American sociology, meant only to be suggestive, bear directly on the mass society theme. For this concept, too, undergoes changes on being transplanted to American soil. To see this most clearly and in more detail, however, we must look once more at European sociology at the turn of the century. More specifically, we shall take note of the work on crowd behavior by social psychologists, primarily French, with an occasional Englishman or Italian or German represented.[7]

---

[6] See, for example, the statement of Rudolf Heberle, cited in Chapter One, n. 2; and cf. Kurt H. Wolff, "Notes Toward a Sociocultural Interpretation of American Sociology," *American Sociological Review*, Vol. 11, pp. 545-553.

[7] We are primarily interested in the work of Gustave Le Bon, Scipio Sighele, Gabriel Tarde and William McDougall. For background material, cf. Fay B. Karpf, *American Social Psychology: Its Origins, Development and European Background* (New York: McGraw-Hill, 1932), and L. L. Bernard, "Crowd," *Encyclopedia of the Social Sciences* (New York: Macmillan, 1935), pp. 612-613.

The Concept of Collective Behavior

This literature on crowds is extremely instructive. A flurry of studies make their appearance in the last decade of the 19th century. They are concerned with the behavior of crowds, and are written by men who consider themselves social scientists. To an unsophisticated eye these studies would appear to have come from nowhere. But this is not so: they are usually inspired by anti-democratic sentiments, and appear to be aimed at discrediting not only the lower orders, with their claims for increased political power through the general franchise, but also in some cases the whole liberal scheme of parliamentarianism. That is to say, these studies are written by men who are not only opposed to the threat to the high *bourgeoisie* from below: some are disenchanted with the *bourgeoisie* themselves, and affect an aristocratic tone in discussing the crowdish tendencies of parliaments. Curiously, the intellectual inspiration for these studies among the French seems in many instances to have come from Taine. His rabid strictures against the mob and its role in the French Revolution, set forth in his *Origins of Contemporary France* (published in 1868), provide many of the examples cited by Le Bon, Tarde, and others.[8]

The tone of these works is anti-liberal, as I have said. The characteristics of "crowds" described by these writers comprise for the most part a catalogue of ugliness and brutality, blind

[8] The decisive influence of Taine is noted by Ethel Shanas, "The Nature and Manipulation of Crowds" (Unpublished M.A. thesis, Department of Sociology, University of Chicago, 1937), pp. 35ff: cf. specifically Gabriel Tarde, *L'opinion et la foule* (Paris: F. Alcan, 1901), pp. 181, 191-92; Gustave Le Bon, *The Crowd* (London: T. F. Unwin, 1896), pp. 21, 71; Scipio Sighele, *Psychologie des sectes* (Paris: Bailliere, 1895), *passim*; William McDougall, *The Group Mind* (Cambridge: Cambridge University Press, 1927), p. 46, all cited by Shanas, *supra*.

It should be noted that the study of the crowd did not proceed without some mutual recriminations on the part of Le Bon and Sighele as to priority. Le Bon published *The Crowd* in 1895 in Paris, and it was translated into English the following year. He had published papers on the subject in 1894. In the preface of Sighele's *La foule criminelle* (Paris: F. Alcan, 1901), however, the author accuses Le Bon of plagiarism. History has given Le Bon the credit for popularizing the study of crowd behavior. See Kimball Young, "Social Psychology," H. E. Barnes (ed.), *History and Prospects of the Social Sciences* (New York: Knopf, 1925), p. 159.

emotion and suggestibility, stupidity and intolerance. While they do not frequently use the term "mass society," they are working into the tradition we have called "the theory of mass society." For Tarde, Le Bon and Sighele, liberalism has torn society apart and produced isolated individuals who now congregate in crowds. The question as to whether or not crowd behavior is observed in all societies, not only those influenced by liberalism, is not raised. Taine's lurid descriptions of the irrationality of the mob during the Terror provide models for both Le Bon and Tarde. Sighele published an Appendix to his *Psychologie des Sectes* containing an essay entitled "Contre le Parliamentarisme," later used by the ideologists of Italian fascism. Electoral crowds, juries and parliaments are given a great deal of attention in this literature. Once these have become identified with "crowds," it is argued that crowd conditions bring about the release of deep prejudices, primitive impulses, racial propensities, and brute instincts. The rationalistic aspect of the liberal faith is attacked by undermining the concept of individual consciousness. In a crowd, "The individual may be brought into such a condition that, having entirely lost his conscious personality, he obeys all the suggestions of the operator who has deprived him of it, and commits acts in utter contradiction with his character and habits."[9] The crowd man "is no longer conscious of his acts. In his case, as in the case of the hypnotized subject, as the same time that certain faculties are destroyed, others may be brought to a high degree of exaltation. Under the influence of suggestion, he will undertake the accomplishment of certain acts with irresistible impetuosity."[10]

People in crowds and their leaders are inclined toward action rather than critical thought. A cultivated individual may become a barbarian in a crowd, a complete creature of instinct. Crowds "are not influenced by reasoning, and can only comprehend rough-and-ready associations of ideas . . . The laws of

[9] Gustave Le Bon, *The Crowd* (London: Ernest Benn, 1947), p. 31.
[10] *Ibid.*

logic have no action on crowds."[11] The clever leader will
affirm what he has said and repeat himself; he will make
assertions, but not employ complex chains of reasoning. To
show that these writers were often speaking of crowd in the
more general sense of "mass," Allport states that both Le Bon
and Sighele maintained that crowd phenomena do not necessarily require physical proximity: "Thousands of isolated individuals may acquire, at certain moments, and under the influence of certain violent emotions,—such for example of a great
national event—the characteristics of a psychological crowd."[12]

An interesting point arises in connection with this literature
on crowds. In his essay, "On Liberty,"[13] John Stuart Mill lists
children and savages as two exceptions to his principle that
each individual is capable of determining what is good for
himself, and that he will know this better than any other.
This is of course a statement of the liberal faith in individual
rationality. In considering the literature on crowds as an attack
on liberalism and parliamentarianism, then, it is interesting
to note that several writers on the crowd compare the behavior
of the individuals in the crowd to that of savages and children,[14] thereby implying their incapacity for self-government.

In the words of McDougall, the crowd is ". . . excessively
emotional, impulsive, violent, fickle, inconsistent, irresolute
and extreme in action, displaying only the coarser emotions

[11] *Ibid.*, p. 112.

[12] *Ibid.*, p. 24. Cf. Gordon W. Allport, "The Historical Background of
Modern Social Psychology," in Gardner Lindzey (ed.), *Handbook of Social
Psychology* (Cambridge: Addison-Wesley, 1953), p. 30. Allport uses the
terms "crowd" and "mass" interchangeably.

[13] J. S. Mill, *Utilitarianism, Liberty, and Representative Government*
(New York: Dutton, 1951), p. 96. "Over himself, over his own body and
mind," declared Mill, "the individual is sovereign." (p. 96.) But this
applies only to "human beings in the maturity of their faculties." Children
are thus excepted, and as for savages, "despotism is a legitimate mode of
government in dealing with barbarians, provided the end be their improve-
ment." (p. 96.)

[14] Cf. Le Bon, *op. cit.*, pp. 36, 114; McDougall, *op. cit.*, p. 45; and
Pascal Rossi, *Les Suggesteurs et la Foule* (Paris: A. Michalon, 1907). Freud
echoes McDougall and Le Bon on this point, in his *Group Psychology and
the Analysis of the Ego* (London: Hogarth, 1922), p. 82.

and the less refined sentiments; extremely suggestible, careless in deliberation, hasty in judgment, incapable of any but the simpler and imperfect forms of reasoning; easily swayed and led, lacking in self-consciousness, devoid of self-respect and of sense of responsibility, and apt to be carried away by the consciousness of its own force, so that it tends to produce all the manifestations we have learnt to expect of any irresponsible and absolute power. Hence its behavior is like that of an unruly child or an untutored passionate savage in a strange situation, rather than like that of its average member; and in the worst cases it is like that of a wild beast rather than like that of human beings."[15]

I do not wish to exaggerate the unanimity of these theorists, or to give a false picture of their view of crowd behavior. Close inspection reveals, as usual, many ambiguities. Le Bon, who certainly does not have a flattering opinion of crowds (he holds them to be a symptom of the decline of civilization) nevertheless declares that crowds may perform acts of great heroism and courage, greater than any of which the individual members would have been capable.[16] Nor is there always agreement on details. While all these crowd theorists agree that the individual possesses the potentiality for crowd action, these impulses are regarded as ordinarily controlled by social norms. Thus crowd behavior is a kind of explosion of repressed impulses.[17] But on the subject of leadership, Tarde holds that a crowd without a leader did not exist, while Le Bon and Sighele hold the opposite view. All may agree on the focus of attention, the emotional rather than the rational qualities, and the suggestibility of crowds, but there is disagreement on the role of mere numbers and of proximity in crowd

[15] McDougall, *op. cit.*, p. 45. The influence of both McDougall and Le Bon is quite evident in Freud's essay (*supra*), in which the latter tried to generalize the results of his study of individual psychopathology to a wide range of groups including crowds, mobs, and religious and military hierarchies.

[16] Le Bon, *op. cit.*, p. 45.

[17] See Roger Brown, "Mass Phenomena" in Gardner Lindzey, *op. cit.*, p. 844. This summary also uses the terms "crowd" and "mass" interchangeably.

behavior. Le Bon tends to view it more as a state of mind, a psychological quality, while Tarde and Sighele stress the group factor.[18]

In spite of these disagreements, however, it should be clear that these students of crowd behavior viewed it as somehow pathological and definitely undesirable. I have cited these Europeans to make more sharp the break with this tradition which occurred in the United States under the aegis of the study of "collective behavior."[19] Now I do not mean to say that there were no Americans who continued the tradition of Le Bon and Tarde and the others. In fact, the American who first wrote a book with the title *Social Psychology*, Edward A. Ross, was profoundly indebted to Tarde. Yet even in the work of Ross the change was clear, although he wrote prior to Park's formulation of the idea of "collective behavior." What was the character of this change?

Lacking a feudal tradition as we have said, and possessing from the beginning a liberal-democratic tradition, the United States does not provide fertile soil for the development of an anti-democratic social psychology of crowds. Anti-parliamentarian rhetoric of the type offered by Sighele falls on deaf ears among American sociologists. There is almost nothing in the nature of published material in American social psychology and sociology in the 20th century which reflects the passionate interest in the crowd on the part of these conservatives who wrote during the last decade of the 19th. The field of "collective behavior," first defined by Robert E. Park in a pioneer textbook in sociology in 1921, is developed in a synoptic article

[18] Cf. Shanas, *op. cit.*, Ch. III. These theorists all borrowed from each other, but sometimes borrowed elements which did not fit into their conceptual schemes.

[19] To indicate the general character of this concept, which will be examined in more detail below, the following quotation from a definitive article may be useful: "The nature of collective behavior is suggested by consideration of such topics as crowds, mobs, panics, manias, dancing crazes, stampedes, mass behavior, public opinion, propaganda, fashion, fads, social movements, revolutions, and reforms." Herbert Blumer, "Collective Behavior," in A. M. Lee (ed.), *Outline of Sociology* (New York: Barnes & Noble, 1946), p. 167. The first edition, edited by Robert E. Park, appeared in 1939.

by Herbert Blumer in 1939. A few articles are published and the field of "collective behavior" is established as part of American social psychology by the time F. B. Karpf publishes her history in 1932,[20] although there are regional variations in the acceptance of the concept. The Department of Sociology at the University of Chicago, for over twenty-five years the center of sociological study in the United States, is also a center for the diffusion of the concept in the training of sociologists under Park, Blumer, and their students. Yet before 1957 there is not a single textbook on this subject published in the United States.[21] Although the fields of sociology and social psychology have been burgeoning during the past several decades, the field of collective behavior has remained more or less static by comparison. Herbert Blumer, in reviewing the state of the field, declares in a recent article: "The field of collective behavior has not been charted effectively.... Although much has been added to our knowledge of separate topics within the last two decades no significant contribution has been made to the general analysis of collective behavior."[22]

Let us examine this literature in a little more detail. The American sociologist Edward A. Ross writes in the tradition of Tarde on the subject of crowds,[23] and deals with fashion, crazes and custom as results of a kind of "multiple suggestion."

[20] *Op. cit.*

[21] See Ralph H. Turner and Lewis M. Killian, *Collective Behavior* (New York: Prentice-Hall, 1957). I exclude such important works as Walter Lippmann's *Public Opinion* and Thurman Arnold's *Folklore of Capitalism* because these men are not in the mainstream of American academic sociology, do not utilize the particular concept in question, and are not primarily concerned with "collective behavior." Their exclusion is arbitrary in the sense that it is dictated by the necessity of limiting this study. But no larger appraisal of the subject in the context of American intellectual history would be complete without a discussion of their influence.

[22] Herbert Blumer, "Collective Behavior," in J. P. Gittler (ed.), *Review of Sociology* (New York: John Wiley & Sons Inc., 1957), p. 127.

[23] See his *Social Psychology* (New York: Macmillan, 1908), and *Social Control* (New York: Macmillan, 1901). An American historian of sociology says that the latter volume "may be regarded, in part, as a free translation of passages from Tarde's *Laws of Imitation*." (F. N. House, *Development of Sociology* [New York: McGraw-Hill, 1936], p. 320.)

Ross, however, does not start a tradition of research and inquiry into crowd behavior in American sociology. He is interesting because he tries to combine theoretical elements which are quite contradictory. Accepting the views of Tarde on imitation and suggestion as the basis of social life, and thus tacitly accepting the irrationalist critique of liberal democratic theory, he still celebrates the bourgeois virtues in his sociology.[24] A few more isolated books appear, none written by American sociologists, on the subject of the crowd prior to Park's statement in 1921. Among these are the works of William Martin Conway,[25] W. Trotter,[26] Boris Sidis[27] and Everett Dean Martin.[28] The last already shows the influence of Freud; and the latter's *Group Psychology and the Analysis of the Ego* is also published in 1921.

The first work which resulted in anything like a tradition of inquiry in the field was undoubtedly that of Park. His interest had been stimulated by studies in Europe, although prior to that time he had had an unusual career as a journalist. Born in Pennsylvania in 1864, Park grew up in a small Minnesota town. He was an undergraduate at the University of Michigan, when he studied under John Dewey. After receiving his degree, he held a succession of jobs as a newspaper reporter and editor in Minneapolis, Detroit, Denver, New York and Chicago, a time during which he undoubtedly de-

---

[24] See *Social Control*, pp. 72, 78-80; *Social Psychology*, pp. 49, 54-56.
[25] William Martin Conway, *The Crowd in Peace and War* (New York: Longmans, 1915).
[26] W. Trotter, *Instincts of the Herd in Peace and War* (New York: Macmillan, 1917).
[27] Boris Sidis, *The Psychology of Suggestion* (New York: Appleton, 1919).
[28] Everett Dean Martin, *The Behavior of Crowds* (New York: Norton, 1921). The following quotation from Brown, *op. cit.*, is an example of how theorists may talk past each other because their concepts have roots in different cultural contexts: "Le Bon had an aristocratic bias which inclined him to equate the lower classes (economically and socially) with the mob . . . To Le Bon, the French Revolution was the beginning of crowd rule. Martin, however, felt that Le Bon overlooked the 'dominant crowd,' the 'crowd which brands everything that opposes its interests as anarchy and Bolshevism.' " (p. 842.)

veloped his feeling for the big city and his flair for urban sociology. Returning to graduate study, Park received his M.A. in psychology at Harvard, where he studied with Munsterberg, Royce and James.

Still unsure of his vocation, Park left the United States for Berlin in 1899, and there listened to the lectures of the great European sociologist Georg Simmel. In 1900 he went to the University of Strasbourg, and heard Wilhelm Windelband. When Windelband went to Heidelberg, in 1903, Park followed him there, and in the following year published his doctoral dissertation, *Masse und Publikum.*[29] In this thesis Park's interest in crowd behavior took formal shape and he tried to establish a distinction between the crowd and the public, which had previously been handled in careless fashion by such thinkers as Sighele. He returned to this field of interest when preparing the textbook in sociology (with Ernest Burgess) fifteen years later.

Unfortunately, Park's definitive statement is a masterpiece of ambiguity. He does not sufficiently distinguish between ordinary social behavior, which is by definition "collective," and the particular kind of behavior which occurs when ordinary social rules and usages break down or are absent from the situation.[30] But we come to the striking aspect of the theory

[29] Robert Ezra Park, *Masse und Publikum* (Bern: Lack and Grunau, 1904). This movement to the Rhineland was symbolic of a larger intellectual movement away from Berlin, the critique of positivism, in which Park may have participated. Windelband's rectoral address in 1894 constituted a "declaration of war against positivism" (H. Stuart Hughes, *Consciousness and Society, op. cit.*, p. 47).

[30] *"Collective Behavior Defined.* A collection of individuals is not always, and by the mere fact of its collectivity, a society. On the other hand, when people come together anywhere, in the most casual way, on the street corner or at a railway station, no matter how great the social distances between them, the mere fact that they are aware of one another's presence sets up a lively exchange of influences, and the behavior that ensues is both social and collective. It is social, at the very least, in the sense that the train of thought and action in each individual is influenced more or less by the action of every other. It is collective insofar as each individual acts under the influence of a mood or state of mind in which each shares, and in accordance with conventions which all quite unconsciously accept, and which the presence of each enforces upon the others . . . In any case . . . even in the

immediately, in the context of a discussion of social unrest: "The most elementary form of collective behavior seems to be what is ordinarily referred to as 'social unrest.' Unrest in the individual becomes social when it is, or seems to be, transmitted from one individual to another, but more particularly, when it produces something akin to the milling process in the herd. . . . The significance of social unrest is that it represents at once a breaking up of the established routine and a preparation for new collective action. Social unrest is of course not a new phenomenon; it is possibly true, however, that it is peculiarly characteristic, as has been said, of modern life. The contrast between the conditions of modern life and of primitive society suggests why this may be true."[31]

There follows a summary paragraph and quotation from Sumner on the characteristics of life in primitive tribes. But Park stresses that the isolation of such local groups has broken down, and changes in one place may now have important consequences thousands of miles away: "The first effect of modern conditions of life has been to increase and vastly complicate the economic interdependence of strange and distant peoples, i.e., to destroy distances and make the world, as far as national relations are concerned, small and tight. The second effect has been to break down family, local and national ties, and emancipate the individual man. . . . A survey of the world today shows that vast changes are everywhere in progress. Not only in Europe but in Asia and Africa new cultural contacts have undermined and broken down the old cultures. The effect has been to loosen all the social bonds and reduce society to its individual atoms. The energies thus freed

---

most casual relations of life, people do not behave in the presence of others as if they were living alone like Robinson Crusoe, each on his individual island. The very fact on their consciousness of each other tends to maintain and enforce a great body of convention and usage which otherwise falls into abeyance and is forgotten. Collective behavior, then, is the behavior of individuals under the influence of an impulse that is common and collective, an impulse, in other words, that is the result of social interaction." (R. E. Park and E. W. Burgess, *Introduction to the Science of Sociology* [Chicago: University of Chicago Press, 1921], p. 865.)

[31] *Ibid.*, p. 866.

have produced a world-wide ferment. Individuals released from old associations enter all the more readily into new ones. Out of this confusion new and strange political and religious movements arise, which represent the groping of men for a new social order."[32]

The important shift which has taken place is that crowds, mobs and masses are no longer being considered as necessarily pathological. There is a change of perspective which has transformed the sociology which Park assimilated in European lecture halls. The phenomena of collective behavior are being interpreted as having a constructive potential, not merely as representing the destruction of civilization—as in the writings of Le Bon. Park, under the acknowledged influence of such late 19th and early 20th century evolutionary concepts as found their way into the work of Spencer and Sumner insists on seeing crowd behavior, "collective behavior," as representing the beginnings of new institutions, new social order, coming into being to fulfill needs which remained unsatisfied under the old. Collective behavior is thus the seedbed, the breeding-ground of new institutions which will satisfy these pent-up needs. There is an implicit judgment on the old institutions: if they were unsatisfactory, then so much the better if they are consigned to the ash heap of history. We are a long way from Le Bon and Tarde with this naturalism. There is a social Darwinist conception here, elaborated in other sections of the book, of the life cycle of institutions. Collective behavior represents the earliest stages of the life cycle. Summarizing his chapter on the crowd and the public, Park declares: "The materials in this chapter have been arranged under the headings: (a) social contagion, (b) the crowd, and (c) types of mass movements. The order of materials follows, in a general way, the order of institutional evolution. Social unrest is first communicated, then takes form in crowd and mass movements, and finally crystallizes in institutions. The history of almost any single social move-

[32] *Ibid.*, p. 867.

ment—women's suffrage, prohibition, Protestantism—exhibits in a general way, if not in detail, this progressive change in character. There is at first a vague general discontent and distress. Then a violent, confused, and disorderly but enthusiastic and popular movement arises. Finally, the movement takes form; develops leadership, organization; formulates doctrine; and dogmas. Eventually it is accepted, established, legalized. The movement dies, but the institution remains."[33]

The idea that the crowd is a kind of elementary grouping, from which the sect issues "like the chick from the egg," Park took from Sighele.[34] But he has combined it with some other ideas which make it completely different from any consideration of crowd behavior among the European theorists. And it should be clear that several important shifts of context have taken place. It is perhaps characteristic of the American sociology of the period between the wars that this problem should now be discussed in terms of process rather than structure, as "behavior" and "action" rather than as a set of fixed categories or relations between the classes. And this process theory is not teleological, as in the case of Marxism, but is almost completely naturalistic and relativistic. There is perhaps an overtone of liberal optimism and faith in progress in this formulation; but primarily it is a sociological reflection of the completely different political and social climate in the United States. This literature on crowds and collective behavior is instructive in that it indicates something of the influence of that climate on the development of American sociology. It is also significant in that the most important formulation of ideas of "mass behavior" by American sociologists takes place within the larger context of the concept of "collective behavior" discussed above.

[33] *Ibid.*, p. 874. Yet Park was unwilling to accept the logical consequences of this naturalistic approach: his Darwinism stopped short of approval of social revolution. See his remarks in the introduction to L. P. Edwards, *The Natural History of Revolution* (Chicago: University of Chicago Press, 1927), pp. ix-xiii.

[34] *Ibid.*, p. 872. Cf. *Psychologie des Sectes*, Paris, 1898, p. 46.

To recapitulate: collective behavior is no longer interpreted by Park as a threat to the established order; there is none of the invective one finds in Le Bon. The "rise of the masses" as signifying the end of civilization is replaced by an evolutionary conception of institutions, in which crowd behavior represents the initial stages. All institutions have such an initial stage, followed by a period of flourishing growth, persistence, and eventual decline. Thus the beginnings of the Methodist church may be found in ecstatic crowd behavior in 18th century England. Park cites two types of crowds: the expressive crowd, which is ecstatic or orgiastic, but does not act toward a common goal; and the acting crowd, which does. The first is exemplified by a revival meeting, the second by a lynch mob. So far as mass behavior was concerned, Park is content to rest on the contributions of Sumner, who makes a rough distinction between "masses" and "classes" in *Folkways*. By "masses" Sumner means the upholders of the mores, a kind of huge middle-class, in his imagery; by classes he means the elites ultimately responsible for innovation.[35] Yet the conceptual framework of "collective behavior" provides room for a theory of mass behavior; and this Park's student, Herbert Blumer, undertakes in an article published in 1935.[36] The author follows the lead of Park and insists on considering mass behavior as elementary collective behavior. Blumer declares that although customary usage has associated "masses" with a single horizontal stratum in society, mass behavior considered as elementary collective behavior is not necessarily identified with any particular layer of society. As in the pragmatic social psychology of Dewey and G. H. Mead, the act

[35] William Graham Sumner, *Folkways* (Boston: Ginn & Co., 1906), pp. 45-53; and Ch. V, *passim*. Sumner's concept of "societal selection," brought into his discussion of fashion phenomena, is an obvious Social Darwinist precursor of the idea of "converging selections" which finds its way into the Park-Blumer theory of mass behavior. Mass phenomena are for Sumner a trial-and-error process leading to the development of the folkways.
[36] Herbert Blumer, "Molding of Mass Behavior Through the Motion Pictures," *Publications of the American Sociological Society*, Vol. 29, 1935, pp. 115-127.

is the locus of study, and thus the mass is here defined in terms of action rather than the position of a specific group in a presumably fixed system of classes.

In Blumer's theory of mass behavior the individuals who comprise the mass come from a wide variety of local cultures; the mass is composed of individuals with heterogeneous backgrounds with regard to social position, occupation, family life, community and local tradition. On the basis of this assumption, Blumer goes on to state that the area of mass behavior is exterior to the realm of the local culture. The objects and experiences which constitute the foci of attention in mass behavior lie outside the local culture of the individuals involved. These points are borne out, declares Blumer, by the rarity of mass behavior in settled folk communities: "In folk communities where the forms and scope of life are ordered, mass behavior scarcely occurs, and when it does occur it represents an excursion from the ways of such folk life. The form of mass behavior, as we are acquainted with it historically, is to be found in a complex heterogeneous society, or in folk societies in a state of disruption."[37]

Having provided the basis for a definition of the mass, Blumer goes on to say that "the concern of mass behavior with objects and interests which transcend the demands and preoccupations made by folk or local culture has both its destructive and its constructive phases." Mass behavior is destructive, in the sense that while it transcends the local culture it represents an attack on it. "Things which catch the attention of the mass represent invasions as well as innovations, experiences which do not arise in the texture of local group life and which are not prescribed by local conventions. Mass influences always detach the individual to some degree from his local group. The area of individual experience in which such influences seem to operate is that which is not satisfied by local life."[38]

[37] Blumer, *op. cit.*, p. 116.
[38] *Ibid.*, p. 117.

In the emphasis on the destructive aspect of mass behavior, may be seen the influence of the European theory of mass society. The individual is seen as alone, bereft of the warmth and security of the primary groups. More important, the mass media, such as the motion picture, are seen as acting on him directly as an isolated individual—not within the context of group interaction.

The constructive phase, however, emphasizes the new approach embodied in Park's formulation of collective behavior: it represents the beginning of efforts to satisfy needs not taken care of by the local culture. This serves to introduce a new organization into that area of life touched by mass behavior.

"The alienation of the individual from his group implies his participation—even though it be poor—in a wider universe. The very fact that the individual's attention is directed away from local group life means that orientation is being made to a larger world, to a wider scope of existence, and, in a measure, to a new order. This point can be understood somewhat better if one recognizes that mass behavior implies that individual dispositions, appetites and wishes are not being satisfied in full by the forms of life in local groups. Mass behavior seems to represent preparatory attempts, however crude they may be, at the formation of a new order of living. It can be thought of as constituting the earliest portion of the cycle of activity involved in the transition from settled folk life to a new social order."[39]

The theory of Blumer thus represents a mixture of European and American elements. Mass behavior represents a disintegration of the local culture, the beginnings of a new order, and the efforts of the individual for a satisfying life not provided in his local culture. Blumer goes on to try to define the nature of mass behavior itself. He sees it as a homogenous aggregate of individuals who, in the mass, are essentially alike, individually indistinguishable. This in spite

[39] *Ibid.*, p. 117.

of the fact that they come from dissimilar local backgrounds and do not know each other.

"This homogeneity of the mass may be expressed also by saying that the individuals in the mass are anonymous and have no designated places. They are anonymous in part because they come from different local groups and social milieux, and, hence, do not know one another. Further, because there is practically no communication or discourse between them. But chiefly because in the mass they do not have any status or accepted position. The mass is not organized like a social group, a society, or a community. It has no settled framework of life, no established forms of social relations, and no allocation of individuals to designated roles. Instead, as all writers seem to agree, it is inchoate and formless. . . . All of this may be stated in a different way by declaring that the mass has no culture, meaning by this that it has no traditions, no established rules or forms of conduct, no body of etiquette adjusting the relations of individuals, and no system of expectations or demands."[40]

In the mass, then, individuals are isolated, anonymous and detached. There is no interaction between them. Yet, paradoxically, they are together, by virtue of their individual attentions' being focused on a common object. But their togetherness is a result of each individual seeking to satisfy his own needs.

"The form of mass behavior, paradoxically, is laid down by individual lines of activity and not by concerted action. . . . These individual lines of action . . . may converge in a startlingly unanimous direction and thus make the behavior of the mass exceedingly effective. But this is not the result of consensus or of mutual understanding. Mass behavior, then, is a congeries of individual lines of action. . . . The mass is likely to be inarticulate. Its dispositions and feelings . . . are likely to be vague and unchannelled, its ideas and images amorphous and confused."[41]

[40] *Ibid.*, pp. 118-119.   [41] *Ibid.*, p. 119.

The selections of the individuals-in-the-mass ultimately converge, thereby giving mass behavior its mass character. These selections, according to Blumer, always offer some possibility of satisfying the vague discontents which are felt on the level of local culture. Such selection is viewed as playing an increasingly important role in modern society—a symptom of shifts of taste, attitudes, interests and, at other levels, of power and influence: "Mass behavior, even though a congeries of individual lines of action, may become of momentous significance. If these lines converge, the influence of the mass may be enormous, as is shown by the far-reaching effects on institutions ensuing from shifts in the selective interest of the mass. A political party may be disorganized or a commercial institution wrecked by such shifts in interest or taste."[42]

A gold rush, the nation-wide sale of a particular dentifrice, the success of a particular film star, may all be analyzed in terms of this model of collective behavior. But the predominant imagery connected with Blumer's theory is still partly European: the idea of large numbers of individuals who have been wrested loose from a stable group life, and who now must face the world without the support of the groups which formerly provided an orientation and habitual basis for action. The new element in the theory is that emphasizing the potentially liberating effects of this breakdown of the older group authority; and this emphasis is properly seen as an expression of the liberal ethos. This positive aspect was stressed by Park, of whom Everett Hughes has written, appropriately: "His real passion was man the struggler—and unlike many of those who have drawn—as he did—a sharp contrast between the city and those communities where life appears to run in safer, smoother channels, Park's choice lay with the city, where, as he put it—every man is on his own."[43]

[42] Herbert Blumer, "Collective Behavior," in A. M. Lee (ed.), *Outline of Sociology* (New York: Barnes & Noble, 1946), p. 186. The part of this article dealing with mass behavior is a condensation of Blumer's 1935 article, *op. cit.*

[43] Everett C. Hughes (ed.), *Human Communities* (Glencoe: Free Press, 1952), p. 6.

But it is precisely this state of affairs which is bemoaned by European theorists of mass society. In man's "being on his own" these theorists see not liberation, but alienation. That very individualism which is symbolized for Americans in the independent farmer of Crèvecour and the westward-moving pioneer, is regarded by the European mass society theorists as a Fall from Grace, as represented by a medieval synthesis, a concept of a "golden age" which historians are now showing to be somewhat questionable even as an "ideal type."

The European theory of mass society is a broad concept, a mystique which aims at characterizing a "whole"; the Park-Blumer theory of mass behavior emphasizes the action of parts or particles. This difference provides an echo of familiar statements on the general differences between European and American sociology. Karl Mannheim, viewing American sociology with European eyes, declared: "American sociology is characterized by its peculiar delight in a form of empiricism which I should be inclined to call an 'isolating empiricism'; for, whilst the enumeration and description of facts becomes always more exact and refined, the constructive bases of social life are completely veiled behind the mass of secondary details. This, it seems, can only be attributed to the fact that the most urgent impulses to the growth of sociological investigation in the United States arose from the immediate problems of everyday life which present themselves in any colonizing society that spreads itself over an expansive territory and has to develop its social institutions in a relatively short span of time. In such a society the most difficult and vital problems crop up one by one, and social study concentrates on the solution of these isolated problems. Here we have one reason for the prevalence in American sociology of questions such as those of gangs, of delinquency, of the conflict of different races living in the same territorial region, of the psychic adjustment of immigrants, all of which are problems that exist in society. The totality of society is veiled because of the general belief that if the difficulties of single institutions and particular institutions are solved in the right way, the entirety of society will reveal itself through a process of integrating the solutions of individual social difficulties."[44]

Mannheim is here insisting that the individualistic liberalism of the American sociologists is a luxury based on the existence of the frontier and a loosely-defined social structure.[45] His critique applied to the work of Park and Blumer is a critique not only of sociology but of American society: an emphasis on the autonomy of individual particles ignores the larger consensus which makes this freedom possible. And it also makes it possible, he implies, for American sociologists to carry on their work without recourse to the concepts of classes and elites, the basic order of the *Standesgesellschaft* which for him both defines society and provides it with an ideal.

Yet, in spite of such differences, the work of Park and Blumer actually contains as much of the old European theory of mass society as it does the new concepts of collective behavior which I have associated with a specifically American context. For in the writings of Park and Blumer there is perpetuated that sociological romanticism which stresses the aloneness of the individual in an urban environment increasingly impersonal and indifferent to his hopes and desires. This is a theme discussed in previous chapters in terms of its political context—19th century conservatism in some instances, Marxism in others—but in all cases, an anti-individualist critique of liberalism. This creates difficulties for a thinker like Park who, as I have indicated, was both a liberal and a sociologist. It helps to account for the contradictions within Park's thought revealed in his writings. Professor Hughes' characterization of Park cited above, emphasizing his individualist-liberal side, is contradicted frequently in the same volume to which his comments constitute an introduction. Park discussed "successful" immigrant groups as being those which main-

[44] Karl Mannheim, "American Sociology," *Essays on Sociology and Social Psychology* (New York: Oxford University Press, 1953), p. 191.
[45] *Ibid.*

tained tight organization in the face of the American success struggle.[46] His imagery here does not emphasize the fact that the individual members of these groups were "on their own," but rather that they were part of close-knit communities which provided the necessary social and affective support; the Jewish and Japanese groups are cited in particular. The hobo, long a symbol of American intransigence and unwillingness to be roped into the struggle for status, is treated by Park as an anachronism: "The hobo is, in fact, merely a belated frontiersman, a frontiersman at a time and in a place when the frontier is passing or no longer exists."[47] Finally, speaking of himself and his fellow-sociologists, he says: "We are encouraging a new parochialism, seeking to initiate a movement that will run counter to the current romanticism with its eye always on the horizon, one which will recognize limits and work within them."[48]

How, indeed, are such statements to be reconciled with Hughes' "romantic" and individualistic image of Park? Yet these are not the only elements of Park's thought which indicate anti-individualistic trends.

Park's concept of the city is marked by a tendency to see everywhere the effort to re-create the conditions of life in the rural village, where everyone knew everyone else—an idyllic *Gemeinschaft* which found a more vivid expression in the imagination of sociologists than in historical fact. In such a view of the city, which still survives in American urban sociology, may be seen the faint outlines of the 19th century precursors of the theory of mass society. Strongly influencing

[46] *Op. cit.*, p. 95.

[47] *Ibid.*, p. 72. If my argument as to the tension between individualist-liberalism and sociology is correct, it should be possible to trace such ambiguities and contradictions in the work of the leading members of the Chicago school of sociology. The same problems, for example, may be found in the writings of Park's student, Louis Wirth. Wirth paradoxically called for the study of consensus as the sociological task *par excellence*, at the same time that he asserted his commitment to a maximization of individual freedom. See Reinhard Bendix, "Social Theory and Social Action in the Sociology of Louis Wirth," *American Journal of Sociology*, Vol. LIX, No. 6, May, 1954.

[48] *Ibid.*

Europeans and Americans on the Crowd

Park's view here is the German romantic sociology of the late 19th century, as exemplified by Tönnies *Gemeinschaft und Gesellschaft* and Georg Simmel's *"The Metropolis and Mental Life"* and *"The Stranger"*;[49] and in Blumer's concept of the isolated, anonymous and detached individual may be seen the persistent parable of alienation that is the theory of mass society.

[49] Kurt H. Wolff (ed.), *The Sociology of Georg Simmel* (Glencoe: Free Press, 1950), pp. 402-424. Cf. *The Philosophy of Money* (Munich and Leipzig: Duncker and Humblot, 1900).

CHAPTER FOUR

THE RISE OF AMERICAN SOCIOLOGY

THE interpretation of American and European sociology offered in the previous chapter stressed the differences in social and political context and the subsequent differences in the rise of sociology itself. In these differences lies part of the explanation for the American critique of the theory of mass society. To trace the development of American sociology, even in outline, is to recognize the historical influences which provided the background for the American critique.

There exists no study which attempts to deal with the history of American sociology from the standpoint of the sociology of knowledge, or as a sustained effort in intellectual history. Of the partial studies and historical sketches which do exist, the best are chapters in books devoted to a larger exposition of sociological material, or articles dealing with a particular trend or school;[1] the worst are close to being mere catalogues of courses and presidents of the American Sociological Society. As most of the historical studies are written by sociologists with a commitment to a particular school or outlook, they are frequently neither circumspect nor impartial. Thus the authors of an otherwise excellent monograph tend to stretch American sociology on the rack of a particularist interpretation, where all theories regardless of content are assimilated to a convergence of underlying values called "voluntaristic nominalism."[2] Another study tends to obscure the character of early 20th century American sociology by implying that many of the early sociologists and their audiences

---

[1] An example is C. Wright Mills, "The Professional Ideology of Social Pathologists," *American Journal of Sociology*, Vol. 49, No. 2, Sept. 1943.

[2] Roscoe C. Hinkle Jr. and Gisela J. Hinkle, *The Development of Modern Sociology* (Garden City: Doubleday, 1954). For a contrary statement, cf. Richard Hofstadter, *Social Darwinism in American Thought* (Boston: Beacon, 1955), pp. 167-169. "It is easier to enumerate the achievements of this renaissance than to characterize its intellectual assumptions, but certainly its leading figures did share a common consciousness of society as a collective whole rather than a congeries of individual atoms."

were members of "the radical Left" in the European sense.[3] Still other accounts are so conventional, so little concerned with gaining any perspective on American sociology, that they are of little value as interpretations and become themselves "the data" for the intellectual historian. Most helpful, however, are the accounts of Shils,[4] Coser,[5] Wirth,[6] Small,[7] the Hinkles,[8] Hofstadter,[9] Page,[10] Faris,[11] Mills,[12] Martindale,[13] and Wolff;[14] also of interest are those of the Bernards,[15] Beal,[16] and Barnes.[17]

[3] Lewis Coser, *The Functions of Social Conflict* (Glencoe: Free Press, 1956) pp. 1-29.

[4] Edward A. Shils, "Sociology in the United States," *Pilot Papers*, June, 1947; and an expanded version, *The Present State of American Sociology* (Glencoe: Free Press, 1948).

[5] *Op. cit.*

[6] Louis Wirth, "American Sociology, 1915-1947," *American Journal of Sociology*, Index to Vol. 1-52, 1895-1947.

[7] Albion Small, *Origins of Sociology* (Chicago: University of Chicago, 1924); and "Fifty Years of Sociology in the United States," reprinted in *American Journal of Sociology*, Index to Vol. 1-52, 1895-1947.

[8] I am especially indebted to the Hinkles' account of the early period of American sociology.

[9] Richard Hofstadter, *The Age of Reform: From Bryan to F.D.R.* (New York: Knopf, 1955) Chapters iv-v; and *Social Darwinism in American Thought, op. cit.*, Ch. 8.

[10] Charles H. Page, *Class and American Sociology: From Ward to Ross* (New York: Dial, 1940). Professor Page's pioneer study in the history of American sociologists' approaches to class has recently been supplemented by Milton M. Gordon, *Social Class in American Sociology* (Durham: Duke University Press, 1958).

[11] Robert E. L. Faris, "American Sociology," *Twentieth Century Sociology* (ed.) Georges Gurvitch and Wilbert E. Moore (New York: Philosophical Library, 1945).

[12] C. Wright Mills, *op. cit.*

[13] Don Martindale, "Prefatory Remarks: The Theory of the City," in Max Weber, *The City* (Glencoe: Free Press, 1958).

[14] Kurt H. Wolff, "Notes Toward a Socio-Cultural Interpretation of American Sociology," *American Sociological Review*, Vol. 11, 1946, pp. 545-553.

[15] L. L. Bernard and Jessie Bernard, *Origins of American Sociology* (New York: Crowell, 1943).

[16] Owen F. Beal, *The Development of Sociology in the United States* (Ann Arbor: Edwards, 1944).

[17] Harry Elmer Barnes, *An Introduction to the History of Sociology* (Chicago: University of Chicago Press, 1948).

That these commentators should differ in their accounts of the beginnings of American sociology is not surprising. But there is a good deal of agreement in spite of the welter of purposes and perspectives represented, particularly on the social and economic setting. Sociology in the United States arose against a background of social change associated with industrialization and urbanization, which, half a century after de Tocqueville, was completely transforming the social and economic landscape which he had surveyed. A wave of social problems, some of them quite new, followed after the settlement of the West and the building of the railroads, the influx of immigrants, the rise of the factory system and the concentration of people in big cities. These comprised the now familiar catalogue of crime, delinquency, divorce, poverty, suicide, alcoholism, minority problems and slums. From many American sociologists these problems evoked a moral response.

The mere fact of the existence of such problems in the United States does not explain the character of this response. It is necessary to examine the ideals of the early sociologists and the social environment from which they were drawn to see this most clearly. If they did not view the gradual eclipse of the small businessman by the "big interests" as evidence of moral progress, if they attacked the robber barons for their lack of concern for the general welfare, for commercialism, greed, and the introduction of false values of conspicuous consumption, they did so from the standpoint of the frontier values of rural simplicity and neighborliness and of a religious concern for the individual. C. Wright Mills has documented this in his essay on American social pathologists, underscoring, for example, Charles Cooley's desire for a return to "primary group communities having Christian and Jeffersonian legitimations" in the face of encroaching urbanization. And the work of men like Edward A. Ross was certainly inspired by compassion for the social and economic difficulties of the small farmer and businessman attending the rise of the industrial and financial combinations and the men who ran them.

"From the farmers' viewpoint, these men had engineered the price decline, subjected them to usurious rates of interest on their mortgages, squeezed them by high freight rates, and fleeced them by fraudulent bond issues. They were often to be seen as the ogres behind the squalor and poverty of the urban slums. Their machinations were blamed for the downward gyrations of the business cycle which endangered the worker's job, for the inundation of immigrant workers who depressed wages or threatened the worker's job, and for the adoption of a more efficient technology which caused the obsolescence of skills."[18]

It is certainly true that the full force of these social dislocations, evident already in the late 19th century, generated widespread public protest and gave rise to a large number of movements dedicated to social, economic, and sometimes, political reform. American sociology was born into an atmosphere, a climate of opinion, heavily infused with the spirit of reform. But how was it that among men who considered themselves scientists, presumably above the battle, these problems were defined and attacked in moral terms?

There are several reasons for the widespread influence of the reform ideology on American sociologists. Four movements which helped create this climate have certainly not been sufficiently studied as sources for the rise of American social science: the Social Science movement, Populism, Progressivism, and the Social Gospel.[19] In connection with the Progressive

[18] Hinkle and Hinkle, *op. cit.*, p. 2.

[19] The Social Science movement is discussed in detail in Bernard and Bernard, *op. cit.* From its beginnings in the 1840's to the 1890's it was concerned with the uses of science in the interest of social reform. The powerful American Economic Association, founded in 1884, was an outgrowth of the Movement, as was its direct descendant, the American Sociological Society, founded in 1905.

For Populism and Progressivism see Richard Hofstadter, *The Age of Reform, op. cit.*; Merle Curti, *The Growth of American Thought* (New York: Harper, 1943), "Formulas of Protest and Reform," pp. 605-632; Ralph Henry Gabriel, *The Course of American Democratic Thought* (New York: Ronald, 1956), Ch. 16, 26; John D. Hicks, *The Populist Revolt* (Minneapolis: University of Minnesota Press, 1931).

For the Social Gospel, see Gabriel, *op. cit.*, Ch. 20; Henry F. May,

movement especially, there is a rich lode for the historian of the social sciences in America. Different interpretations of the movement provide a stumbling block here. Some historians emphasize the extent to which the movement stressed the general welfare, the public interest, and see in it a foreshadowing of what they regard as the democratic socialism of the New Deal. Others stress the extent to which it was committed to liberal-individualist goals in its attempt to reverse the trend toward bigness and guarantee a fair running of what Professor Hartz calls the Alger race. A definitive answer to the question of whether American sociologists fell into the first camp or the second must wait for a larger study, but there is a good deal of evidence to support the latter view. Sociologists in the early period often took great pains to distinguish themselves from the Socialists, though there were some notable exceptions. There is a sense in which they did not need to, since there were many home-grown reform philosophies—some with roots in Europe to be sure, but distinctive American products nevertheless.

"One of the reasons for the American neglect of Marx was the fact that this country was breeding its own native substitutes in the persons of such naturalistic social scientists as Lewis Henry Morgan, Lester F. Ward, Thorstein Veblen, William Graham Sumner, and Charles A. Beard. As a result of their labors, the new disciplines of anthropology, economics, government, and sociology, at the formative period of their most rapid expansion, were given a strongly naturalistic bent. Theory and practice, however, were seldom abreast of one another. Lewis Henry Morgan, who was a stern, conventional, upstate New York capitalist Labor-hater and fanatical dry, offered the ironic spectacle of delighting Friedrich Engels with a pioneer classic of anthropology, *Ancient Society*, writ-

---

Protestant Churches and Industrial America (New York: Harper, 1949); and Walter Rauschenbusch, *Christianity and the Social Crisis* (New York: Macmillan, 1907).

ten 'in a manner that might have been used by Marx himself.' "[20]

The cry for social justice was being raised on all sides, and whether the cure was in terms of Greenbacks, Christian Socialism or the Single Tax, whether muckraker, Progressive or Knight of Labor, all called attention to existing evils in the cities and in the countryside. Naturalism, evolutionism, transcendentalism, materialism, idealism, historicism, and Social Darwinism in its reformist and conservative variants, when blended together in different combinations, however inconsistent, could provide the scientific weapon which sociologists hoped to use in the struggle against social evil. But they did not, by and large, see America as another vaster Europe, with a class struggle and an exploiting bourgeoisie oppressing the proletarian masses. If they sometimes wrote as if a collectivist society were the answer to American social problems, they did not often write as revolutionaries or even as Socialists. They were engaged in a search for community of the type already discussed in Chapter Two, but they were the products of a liberal milieu. Though their key concepts were often expressions of a demand for a new social order,[21] the individual was often the vehicle for their reform idealism, and here they were often quite inconsistent. Marxism, for example, had little influence on them. Rather, the early sociologists, small town and farm boys almost to a man, faced these problems in moral terms inherited from their social and religious backgrounds. The reform philosophy had penetrated the backwoods, and those who stood ready to heed its moral message were predominantly from rural and religious milieux.

[20] Harold A. Larrabee, "Naturalism in America," in Y. Krikorian (ed.), *Naturalism and the Human Spirit* (New York: Columbia University Press, 1944), p. 350.

[21] The sociological ideal of order haunts even the individualistic Cooley, who sounds like a 20th century Saint-Simon when he answers his own question about the ethical aims of society with the assertion that they are "simply rational aims, representing the ideal of efficient total organization." *Sociological Theory and Social Research* (New York: Henry Holt, 1930), p. 258.

The Rise of American Sociology

"The vast majority of eminent sociologists prior to 1920 came from rural and religious environments. Of the nineteen presidents of the American Sociological Society who had been born prior to 1880, who had completed their graduate studies before 1910, and who had achieved some prominence before 1920, not one had experienced a typically urban childhood. Although some of these sociologists can hardly be identified with an endorsement of the ideology and practices of conventional, institutionalized religion of their era, they were almost without exception fundamentally concerned with ethical issues. . . . Often their reformism was a secular version of the Christian concern with salvation and redemption and was a direct outgrowth of religious antecedents in their personal lives. Lester F. Ward's maternal grandfather and Franklin H. Giddings' and William I. Thomas' fathers had been ministers; William G. Sumner, Albion Small, George E. Vincent, Edward C. Hayes, James P. Lichtenberger, Ulysses G. Weatherly, Charles A. Ellwood, and John L. Gillin had themselves had earlier ministerial careers."[22]

In the light of this recurring combination of rural background and religious ideals it is not surprising, as the Hinkles point out, that these men were to become champions of reform. Nor is it surprising that the Middle West, and not the East, proved the more congenial to the expansion of sociology in the universities;[23] that urbanism and industrialism became the focus for an approach to "social problems"; and that the early sociologists were high-minded reformers in a tradition of secularized Protestantism who championed the values of the small town against the sins of the big city.

Professor Richard Hofstadter offers a supplementary interpretation of the rise of the social sciences in America. He views

[22] Hinkle and Hinkle, *op. cit.*, p. 3.
[23] The hegemony of the Middle West came to an end symbolically only in 1937, when, after a long struggle in the American Sociological Society, the *American Journal of Sociology*—controlled by the department at the University of Chicago—was replaced by the Eastern-based *American Sociological Review* as the official journal of the Society.

the period of the last three decades of the 19th century as the beginning of a status revolution in the United States. The status revolution was most obvious in the contrast between the old established families and the "new men" who were the chief beneficiaries of the industrial transformation. But the most conspicuous losers in the status revolution, according to Hofstadter, were the clergy. The secularization of American society which accompanied the changes in financial and industrial life was reflected in the extent to which judgments of the clergy seem to carry less weight. Religion itself was under attack from the new evolutionary ideas in biology and their extensions in social philosophy. The clergy were being replaced in their capacity as moral and intellectual leaders, as those responsible for higher education, and as bastions of the community with the support of the working classes. The newer, more secular universities that were being founded by the "new men" had social scientists on their faculties with evolutionary science at their command, while the ministers remained with what appeared to many to be anachronistic creeds. Hofstadter's conclusion provides an interesting hypothesis on the origins of American sociology: "In the light of this situation, it may not be unfair to attribute the turning of the clergy toward reform and social criticism not solely to their disinterested perception of social problems and their earnest desire to improve the world, but also to the fact that as men who were in their own way suffering from the incidence of the status revolution they were able to understand and sympathize with the problems of other disinherited groups."[24]

However, Hofstadter is forced to deal with the problem presented by the fact that both the clergy and the professors were in the vanguard of the Progressive movement. If he explains the presence of the clergy in terms of their response to the tensions of downward social mobility, how does he explain the presence of the professors? Here he has recourse to an omnibus explanation, to the effect that "tensions are

[24] Hofstadter, *The Age of Reform, op. cit.*, p. 151.

heightened both in social groups that are rising in the social scale and in those that are falling."

"The situation of the professors is in striking contrast to that of the clergy—and yet the academic man arrived by a different path at the same end as the cleric. While the clergy were being in a considerable measure dispossessed, the professors were rising. The challenge they made to the *status quo* around the turn of the century, especially in the social sciences, was a challenge offered by an advancing group, growing year by year in numbers, confidence, and professional standing. Modern students of social psychology have suggested that certain social-psychological tensions are heightened both in social groups that are rising in the social scale and in those that are falling; and this may explain why two groups with fortunes so varied as the professoriat and the clergy gave so much common and similar support to reform ideologies."[25]

While this theory may explain too much, it does give some idea of the social context and suggests that the motivation of those who passed from religious to secular reform preoccupations and from the clergy to academic sociology were quite complex.

But the academic context itself helps to explain many of the unique characteristics of American sociology. P. A. Sorokin, writing in 1929, observed in retrospect: "American sociology has grown up as a child nursed by the Universities and Colleges: while in Europe its modern start, since Auguste Comte, and development have in a considerable degree taken place outside of the Universities and Colleges."[26]

The fact that the social and professional context of the discipline was provided by the colleges and universities did have important consequences for its development. One critic holds that the rapid expansion of sociology in the universities was due to the decay of the classical and humanistic studies,

[25] *Ibid.*, p. 152.
[26] Pitirim A. Sorokin, "Some Contrasts of Contemporary European and American Sociology," *Social Forces*, Vol. 8, 1929, p. 57.

the creation of a kind of cultural vacuum: "More than half a century has now elapsed since American sociology came into the world. It developed at a time of the decay of classical and humanistic studies, at a time when specialization on the one hand and public disregard on the other were undermining the central position which these studies had once enjoyed in the academic world.

"It was the loosening of their standards and their loss of self-esteem which diminished their power of resistance against a new and unconventional subject, and which permitted the intrusion of sociology into the American university. There were of course demands for it within the university from dissatisfied elements in the economics and political science departments, and pressure for it outside the university from reformers and social workers. But the very condition of its birth and the process of selection which accompanied it meant that sociologists would lack the sense of the past, the traditional intellectual discipline which distinguished the academic man of the late 19th century."[27]

Professor Shils offers no evidence for this unusual interpretation. Possibly he is exaggerating the quality of humanistic scholarship among the academic men of America in the late 19th century. In any case he is being unnecessarily Burkean here; "traditional" standards of judgment are not necessarily the best standards, especially in the history of American academic life.[28]

Far more important than this was the fact that sociologists felt compelled to struggle to establish themselves in the face of the older, more respected social sciences. At the same time they had to try to refute charges, sometimes justified, that they considered their science to be the queen of the social sciences, the "science of sciences."[29] Louis Wirth has com-

[27] Shils, *The Present State of American Sociology, op. cit.*, p. 2.
[28] See R. Hofstadter and W. P. Metzger, *The Development of Academic Freedom in the U. S.* (New York: Columbia University Press, 1955), Chapters 5, 6, 9.
[29] Faris, *op. cit.*, pp. 541-542.

mented on the troubled preoccupations of sociology in the early period, oscillating between delusions of grandeur and feelings of inferiority. Even as late as 1915, he writes, sociologists felt it necessary to try to differentiate themselves from other social scientists. This reflected on part of their own past history, the days of Comte, Spencer and Ward, when sociology was another name for the whole of the social sciences. But during the first decade of the 20th century, when sociologists were struggling for recognition as the practitioners of a specialized discipline, such a definition was clearly inadequate. There were two roads open to sociologists: either they could claim an autonomous, specialized subject matter for themselves, or they could claim the whole of social life as their field of study and justify themselves as an academic department by their efforts to understand social life from a special viewpoint.

"The attempt to legitimize sociology in academic circles on the ground that it had a subject matter of its own left to sociology, as Small put it, the unenviable role of studying the trivial and neglected aspects of the social world which were regarded as too insignificant to merit the attention of political scientists and economists. It meant, essentially, that the sociologists would have to feed on the crumbs that dropped off the table of these better established academic disciplines. The almost exclusive initial preoccupation of sociologists with such topics as poverty, delinquency and crime, insanity, marriage and divorce, slums and other pathologies, together with such subjects as the community, voluntary groups, classes and races, which did not fit so readily into the frames of reference of the state or the market, attests to the correctness of this view.

"Sociologists could not, however, be content for long in their humble position as devotees of a science of leftovers. Nor could the need for adjustment to and securing status in the American academic hierarchy, not to speak of the internal strain toward consistency, fail to generate grave dissatisfaction among the more logical thinkers in the field with the state of sociology as an *omnium gatherum*. As is often the case among those who are afflicted with the Cinderella complex, there developed among a goodly number of sociologists the aspiration to assume the role of generalissimo of the social sciences. Wherever these delusions of grandeur developed, however, they were soon met by rebuffs which in turn led to a reconsideration of the proper scope of sociology and its place among the sciences. This reflection has been proceeding uninterruptedly ever since."[30]

Periodization is always somewhat arbitrary, but several writers agree that the appearance in 1883 of Lester Ward's *Dynamic Sociology* marks the beginning of sociology in this country. The first period in American sociology ends, according to the perspective of the writer, in 1915, with the publication of Robert Ezra Park's essay on the city,[31] or in 1918, with the end of the First World War. The men of the first period shared certain perspectives and methodological presuppositions. Shils describes the "first generation" of American sociologists, chiefly Lester Ward, Franklin Giddings, and Albion Small, as "men of learning and synthetic disposition," system-building theoreticians on the 19th century model. Other accounts provide different divisions of the "generations." Thus Coser, in the context of an inquiry into the uses of the concept of conflict, discusses seven of the dominant figures of early sociology, describing them as "the founding fathers": besides Ward, Giddings and Small, he includes Edward A. Ross, Thorstein Veblen, Charles H. Cooley, and William Graham Sumner. Several of these latter figures are described by Shils as members of the "second generation." There is general agreement, in spite of such differences, that the perspectives of American sociologists were dominated by certain specific presuppositions from the time of Ward's writings beginning in

---

[30] Wirth, *op. cit.*, pp. 276-277.

[31] Robert E. Park, "The City: Suggestions for the Investigation of Human Behavior in the Urban Environment," *American Journal of Sociology*, March, 1915. This essay laid down the lines for a program of empirical research that was to dominate the second period in American sociology and which would mark the hegemony of the Chicago School.

the 1880's to the period around 1915-1918. Albion Small summarized these in a paper presented at the first official meeting of the American Sociological Society in 1906.[32]

"In brief, Small confirmed the general acceptance of four major assumptions among American sociologists of 1906: (1) They accepted the task of searching for scientific laws of human behavior, which resemble invariant *natural laws* governing physical and organic phenomena. (2) They identified social change as social evolution and interpreted it as *progress* toward a better society. (3) They regarded such upward human development as subject to acceleration by direct human *melioristic intervention*, using knowledge of sociological laws. (4) Finally, they conceived of social behavior and society as constituted of *individual behavior* and particularly emphasized the motivations of individuals in association."[33]

This is a fair statement if interpreted in the broadest possible way; it does not do justice to the views of specific thinkers. The emphasis on melioristic intervention would not apply to Sumner in the same way in which it would apply to Lester Ward; and while the emphasis on individual behavior as a focal point of analysis might fit Ward, it would not do for Sumner, Giddings and others. In general, however, the dominant trend in the first period, with the obvious exception of Sumner,[34] is toward a liberal sociology of change and process,

[32] Albion W. Small, "Points of Agreement Among Sociologists," *Publications of the American Sociological Society*, I, pp. 55-71, 1907.

[33] Hinkle and Hinkle, *op. cit.*, pp. 8-9. Looking back at the achievements and shortcomings of the first generation, Albion Small testified in 1924: ". . . A humiliating proportion of the so-called sociology of the last thirty years in America, both inside and outside of the goodly fellowship of scholars who were self-disciplining themselves and one another into the character of scientific specialists, has been simply old-fashioned opinionativeness under a new-fangled name. This confession is in the nature of a purgatorial experience in qualifying for salvation." *Origins of Sociology* (Chicago: University of Chicago Press, 1924), p. 350.

[34] The historian C. Vann Woodward has cited the role of the sociology of Sumner and Giddings in lending strength to Southern segregationist arguments. See *The Strange Career of Jim Crow* (New York: Oxford, 1957), pp. 88-89.

rather than one of conservation and equilibrium. This becomes even more true as we come to the second period.

The second period may be defined roughly as that between the two World Wars. The distinguishing features of this period are an expansion of academic sociology, a large increase in the number of students and faculty, the beginnings of specialization and differentiation within sociology, the search for a methodology which would guarantee the scientific status of the discipline, and the concentration of leadership in research and theory in the Department of Sociology at the University of Chicago.

Shils cites W. I. Thomas, Robert Ezra Park, Charles Horton Cooley, and Edward A. Ross as the dominant figures of the "second generation." These men stood "midway between the sociology of the library and learned meditation on the one hand and the increasingly circumspect research techniques of the present day on the other."[35] All of them were in fact concerned with making sociology more scientific and less speculative. This affected them at the level of values as well as that of methodology, for it was during the second period that the theories of the European irrationalists became more widely known in the United States.[36] The war itself had proved disillusioning to many who had been previously convinced that men are rational to an extent that an increase in knowledge could not help but result in moral progress. Together with a belief in progress, which many could not discard completely, the sociologists of the second generation tried to shed the speculative tradition of the great system-builders and attempted to ground their science in empirical research. Louis Wirth, himself a student of the second-generation at the University of Chicago, has given an excellent account of the major features of this effort: "The development of sociology from 1915 to the present seems to follow suc-

[35] *Pilot Papers, op. cit.,* p. 8.
[36] See H. Stuart Hughes, *Consciousness and Society: The Reorientation of European Social Thought, 1890-1930* (New York: Knopf, 1958), p. 429.

cessive phases of a cycle. Beginning with an interest in the practical problems of everyday life, sociology, under pressure of the quest for respectability and academic legitimation, moved into an era of excessive concern with building up a technical vocabulary and finding rationalizations for systems of classifications and other abstract categories of thought. This led to the emergence of a cult of unintelligibility and increasing remoteness from the concrete reality of the social world. As a result of widespread and often justified bitter criticism from academic and especially journalistic quarters, as well as a growing sense of irrelevance and futility on the part of sociologists themselves, there followed a period of fact-gathering and intensive, but more or less aimless, study of small and often disconnected 'problems' and the immersion into the development of super-refined techniques for ordering and summarizing the crude data thus gathered. While this accumulation of mountains of authentic but meaningless facts and the invention of complicated scientific gadgets for processing these crude data in a more or less mechanical fashion lent a certain aura of pseudo-scientific glamour to the sociologists engaged in it, it obviously lacked the sense of values and hence of direction of the older, philosophically more sophisticated, speculative sociology, while at the same time it yielded a minimum of either practically useful or scientifically generalizable conclusions."[37]

One of the fruits of this new orientation was the intensive study of urban life carried out by Robert E. Park and his students at the University of Chicago. Using concepts borrowed from biology and botany, Park and his associates studied the city from the standpoint of human ecology, distinguishing "natural areas" within which certain social phenomena were normally distributed. The traditional social problems were studied in the context of both the biological, unplanned, "natural" order, and the social, purposeful, moral

[37] Wirth, *op. cit.*, p. 274.

order; the city was the result of the interplay of these two. Between 1915 and 1925 Park, with the collaboration of his associates, notably Ernest Burgess and R. D. McKenzie, directed a series of research projects which, in their published form,[38] stand as a typical example of the work of the second generation. This was the ecological theory of the city. Burgess contributed the concentric zone hypothesis, a theory of the growth and physical expansion of the city, and its differentiation in space; McKenzie stated the "laws" which operated to establish these spatial differentiations.

"Ecology was that phase of biology studying plant and animal forms as they exist in nature in relation to each other and to their environments. Human ecology was a parallel study of the spatial and temporal relations of humans as affected by the social environment. Society was thought to be made up of individuals territorially distributed by competition and selection. Human institutions are accommodated to spatial relations. As these spatial relations change social relations are altered, producing social and political problems."[39]

In Professor Martindale's terse prose one may sense the tough-minded attitudes of the Chicago sociologists, intent on discovering the laws of social life in order to be able to predict and ultimately control the problems of urban existence. The research program laid out by Park and carried on by his successors resulted in the production of an enormous amount of research on urban life, race relations, delinquency, divorce, social disorganization, mass communications and other fields. We may take it as typical of the second-generation effort in sociology. New ground was broken, new fields were staked out, much empirical research was carried out within the framework of a loosely defined theory. The ghetto, the Gold Coast, the slum; the jackroller, the hobo, the hotel-dweller; the gang, the suicide, the delinquent—all provided grist for the mill of the Chicago sociologists. Yet Louis Wirth—"a charter

---

[38] R. E. Park, Ernest W. Burgess, Roderick D. McKenzie, *The City* (Chicago: University of Chicago Press, 1925).

[39] Martindale, *op. cit.*, p. 24.

member of urbanism incorporated" as Martindale calls him—writing in 1938, had this to say about the efforts of the second generation in studying the city: "In the rich literature on the city we look in vain for a theory of urbanism presenting in a systematic fashion the available knowledge concerning the city as a social entity. We do indeed have excellent formulations of theories on such special problems as the growth of the city viewed as a historical trend and as a recurrent process, and we have a wealth of literature presenting insights of sociological relevance and empirical studies offering detailed information on a variety of particular aspects of urban life. But despite the multiplication of research and textbooks on the city, we do not as yet have a comprehensive body of competent hypotheses which may be derived from a set of postulates implicitly contained in a sociological definition of the city, and from our general sociological knowledge which may be substantiated through empirical research."[40]

It is beyond the scope of this chapter to deal with the many contributions of the Chicago School, of the work of W. I. Thomas on life-histories, of W. F. Ogburn in the field of social and cultural change, of George Herbert Mead in the symbolic interactionist social psychology, of Ellsworth Faris' critique of instinct theory, or of the contributions of their many associates and disciples. Sociology is what it is today partly because of their efforts. Nor should I give the impression that no work was being done in sociology which did not derive its inspiration from Chicago. The Chicago School is merely representative of the state of affairs in American sociology between the wars, which led observers like Sorokin to comment: "The bulk of the sociological works in America are marked by their quantitative and empirical character while the bulk of the sociological literature of Europe is still marked by an analytical elaboration of concepts and definitions; by a philosophical and epistemological polishing of words."[41]

---

[40] Louis Wirth, "Urbanism as a Way of Life," *American Journal of Sociology*, Vol. 44, 1938, p. 8.
[41] Sorokin, *op. cit.*, p. 60.

What was the content of the shift in values among the second generation which accompanied the shift in methodology? I have already indicated that the optimistic faith in progress shared by many members of the first generation was discarded, or at least survived in considerably attenuated form, among the men of the second period. Their interest in non-rational factors in human behavior did not compel them to embrace irrationalism and anti-liberal political doctrines. As rational students of non-rational behavior, many of them remained interested in "reform." But such concepts must not be allowed to blur the picture. To be sure, such figures as Park in his identification with the Negro's struggle for status, Ogburn in his diagnosis of a "cultural lag" behind technological advances, and W. I. Thomas in his statement of the aim of sociology as "the abolition of war, of crime, of drink, of abnormality, of slums, of this or that kind of unhappiness"[42] are readily identified with "reform." But such an idea can mean different things to different generations, and indeed, it has meant different things to the various commentators on the history of American sociology.

It was not the "conservative" liberalism of a Sumner which emerged as the characteristic social and political philosophy of American sociologists. Rather, it was an ambiguous philosophy which we have previously described in connection with thinkers like Park, who were liberals and yet at the same time stressed group cohesion, status and consensus in their sociology in a way which was reminiscent of older, conservative thinkers of the 19th century.[43] The sociologists of the second generation

[42] W. I. Thomas, "The Persistence of Primary Group Norms in Present-Day Society and Their Influence in Our Educational System," Herbert S. Jennings *et al.*, *Suggestions of Modern Science Concerning Education* (New York: Macmillan, 1917), p. 197.

[43] Behice Boran, in a Marxist critique of American sociology, has attacked Park and other members of the second generation for stressing "in-groups and out-groups, crowds and masses" rather than class and class conflict. "Social interaction," the author declares, "has been conceptualized as competition and conflict, accommodation and assimilation, to the exclusion of patterns of inter-class conflict in economic, political and other social spheres.

were often "unconscious" liberals who were concerned over the "disorganizing" aspects of American life under the impact of industrialism and urbanism. They were often as unaware of their liberalism, their fundamental assumptions about equality of opportunity, individualism and democracy, as they were of the conservative implications of some of the concepts they employed to analyze the society around them. C. Wright Mills has shown, for example, how American "social patholo-gists" developed an ideology which applied middle-class, small town norms to the phenomenon of change associated with industrialism, emerging with medical analogies and equilibrium[44] concepts which implied that all change was undesirable. They did not resolve the problems raised by their liberalism in conflict with their conservative sociological concepts; rather, these problems remained submerged beneath the liberal consensus which could permit a prominent sociolo-gist to write, as late as 1945: "Although the political attitudes of sociologists in the United States probably cover about the same range as those of the American public, there is no cleav-age of sociology into radical and conservative wings, or into communist and fascist sociologies. The political attitudes of a scholar are generally considered irrelevant to his research, and in most cases are not widely known, even among col-

---

Such a non-committing terminology was functional for sociology in per-mitting it to avoid embroilment in political controversy." "Sociology in Retrospect," *American Journal of Sociology*, Vol. 52, January 1947, p. 312. Professor Coser, however, in the context of a neo-Marxist analysis, *praises* Park because he allegedly made the idea of conflict a center of his system (Coser, *op. cit.*, pp. 19-20). Park's interest in social conflict, however, reflects his Social Darwinism rather than socialist ideology, though he was familiar with socialist writings. But these differences of interpretation demonstrate the difficulty of assigning an original and complex thinker like Park to a pigeonhole based on European categories.

[44] Mills, "The Professional Ideology of Social Pathologists," *op. cit.* The work of Mills himself, notably in *The Power Elite* (New York: Oxford University Press, 1956), is certainly in the populist tradition. This tradi-tion has ideological elements which lend themselves to a *rapprochement* with the theory of mass society. See also, for example, Floyd Hunter, *Top Leadership U. S. A.* (Chapel Hill: University of North Carolina Press, 1959).

leagues who are personally acquainted with him. The American Sociological Society contains a small group of enthusiasts who make constant attempts to commit the Society to political resolutions, but these notions are invariably and decisively rejected, even though the political sympathies of the membership as persons and citizens may often be with the resolution. The adopted policy is to keep separate the roles of sociologist and citizen, of research specialist and political advocate.

"This point of view may have several explanations. Although it is not quite true that the American people do not take politics seriously, there is a certain national practice of applying some of the detachment which is also characteristic of so many American sport activities. The game is played hard, and played to win, but the opponent is not an enemy, and no grudges are to be held. Friendships are not to be made or broken along the lines of this form of conflict. To the majority of Americans the intensity of political sentiment in some European regions looks unsportsmanlike and ridiculous."[45]

It is the vast consensus, the widespread American agreement on fundamentals in politics to which the above quotation points. It is a luxurious liberalism which is described with such a lack of self-consciousness by Faris. If by "the political attitudes of a scholar" he means a preference for the Democratic or the Republican party, this would hardly represent meaningful political choice to a German or a Frenchman. American sociologists have often shared in the unconscious liberalism of their fellow-citizens, oblivious to the social and political strife, the bitter regional and class warfare and ideological struggle which divide their European colleagues in such an "unsportsmanlike" way.

Attitudes such as the one indicated above should make it easier to see that the American critique of the theory of mass society was not the result of a process of self-conscious ideological opposition on the part of American sociologists. Indeed, their general adherence to the doctrine of "value-free" science

[45] Faris, *op. cit.*, pp. 548-549.

would have prevented such an explicitly ideological development. Yet such opposition, culminating in the critique I have indicated, is none the less real for being carried on tacitly or unwittingly.

The period with which we shall be primarily concerned in the following chapter is the one which begins just prior to the Second World War, when many of the "third generation" were rising to maturity as scholars, and the influence of the second generation, though still strong, was beginning to fade. American sociologists had become increasingly conscious of methodological problems, and the work of R. M. MacIver, Louis Wirth, Herbert Blumer, Robert K. Merton, Robert S. Lynd, Arnold Rose and others was to result in a contraction of the field in the effort to deal with hypotheses which were amenable to verification by empirical research procedures, and which were, at the same time, relevant to significant problems and which did not sink into triviality. Louis Wirth observed this trend as early as 1947, even before Robert K. Merton had suggested that sociologists abandon both meaningless empiricism and the construction of cathedral-like systems in favor of "theories of the middle range."[46]

"In recent years sociology seems to have begun to move into a phase closely resembling the period of initial enthusiasm for sociology in America. This phase is marked by a return to the original interest of sociologists in the actual problems of man in society. The presently emerging orientation of sociology differs from that of a generation ago, however, in several important respects; in Small's day the passion for solving the practical problems of society was supported and sustained by little more than the faith that sociology could discover a scientific foundation for ethics and social policies and was guided in its investigations largely by improved but intuitively plausible broad philosophical notions concerning human nature, the social order, and social dynamics.

[46] Robert K. Merton, *Social Theory and Social Structure* (Glencoe: Free Press, 1949), p. 5.

"The contemporary return of sociology to the original interest of its intellectual progenitors in contrast is distinguished by more tempered expectations. . . . Rather than aspiring to the role of the value-setter for society, the contemporary sociologist is increasingly sensitive to the fact that science, or at least science alone, cannot set values."[47]

This third period in American sociology, roughly from 1940 to the present, saw a continuation of some of the processes of increasing specialization and differentiation within the field which had been promoted by the second generation. It was a time of even greater expansion; whole new areas of inquiry were opened up, the number of publications increased, new books in the field multiplied, and an increasing number of sociologists were employed by other institutions than the academic—in government and in business.[48] The Hinkles claim that a shift occurred toward an emphasis on making sociology useful to society rather than stressing its theoretical, abstractly scientific character.[49] This should not be taken to imply that American sociologists tended to give up the effort to measure and to quantify; statistical methods and approaches became very important during the third period. New journals, regional associations and specialized societies grew up, and new interests reflected some changes in American society itself: concern with the sociology of marriage and the family, social psychiatry, industrial sociology, communications and public opinion, medical sociology, aging and retirement, and the study of small groups. The older interests in "reform," reflecting concern with the traditionally defined "social problems," tended to be relegated to special studies, such as that of criminology, or to be institutionally separated through the development of separate schools for social workers. A new range of problems was gradually replacing the old as the question of poverty, for example, was reduced in importance by compari-

[47] Wirth, *op. cit.*, pp. 274-275.
[48] See Hans L. Zetterberg, "A Guide to American Sociology, 1945-55," *Sociology in the United States of America* (Paris: UNESCO, 1956).
[49] Hinkle and Hinkle, *op. cit.*, p. 44.

son with the problems of the growth of bureaucracy and extensive government control in many previously unregulated areas of life. The rise of an enormous middle class, the increase in leisure time, the expansion of great suburban areas, were part of a national picture which led some social scientists to stress the dangers of conformism and to focus on the social implications of de Tocqueville's warnings concerning the tyranny of the majority.[50] But this was a characteristically *liberal* insight, a concern over the decline of individualism. European theories of mass society, often biased against liberalism, did not lend themselves to analysis of these phenomena. And what I have referred to as the conservative character of many sociological concepts prevented many sociologists from dealing with the changes which were taking place in American society before their very eyes.

[50] The work of David Riesman is outstanding in this respect: cf. *The Lonely Crowd* (New York: Doubleday Anchor, 1953), and *Individualism Reconsidered* (Glencoe: Free Press, 1954). Cf. also William H. Whyte, *The Organization Man* (New York: Doubleday Anchor, 1956). It is quite significant that neither of these men were trained in graduate schools of sociology.

CHAPTER FIVE

THE AMERICAN CRITIQUE OF THE THEORY OF MASS SOCIETY: RESEARCH IN MASS COMMUNICATIONS

IT was during the third period in American sociology that the research on mass communications with which we shall be concerned took place. The historical influences discussed in the previous chapter were important factors in the movement toward the kinds of empirical studies which provided the basis for the critique of the mass society concept. We should keep in mind the academic as well as the social and political context. The particular set of American conditions discussed above gave rise to an interest in mass communications research of an empirical character rather than to philosophical reflections on "mass society." Professor Merton has discussed the distinctive European and American forms of inquiry in this respect; he identifies the sociology of knowledge as the European field of which mass communications research is the American variant.[1] What happened from the standpoint of the American sociologists themselves was that empirical research on mass communications revealed that European imagery on the subject of mass society was questionable, at least insofar as it was concerned with the mass media and their audiences. In this area, the American researchers felt that they had "the facts"; and the most important of these facts may be described as a rejection of the image of the isolated, anonymous, detached individual-in-the-mass, in favor of an individual who receives the messages of the mass media within a social context.

In order to understand this shift we must first take note of a general trend in sociological research which has been

[1] Robert K. Merton, *Social Theory and Social Structure* (Glencoe: Free Press), 1949; Part III, Introduction.

called "the rediscovery of the primary group."[2] This movement has been called a "rediscovery" in view of the historical
link with sociologists of the second generation, like Charles H.
Cooley, who first used the term "primary group." Cooley
represented the tradition of social criticism of the impact of
industrialism discussed in the previous chapter. In some respects it represents a return, also, to the ideology of the
"social pathologists" such as Cooley who were concerned
with social disorganization. This shift to the study of small
groups and away from problems connected with the larger
institutional structure is itself not without significance. It is in
part the result of the movement described by Professor Wirth
as a sort of retrenchment, a concern for more limited studies
employing hypotheses which are amenable to verification by
empirical research. It also reflects an increasing concern with
the "forms of association," as Simmel called them; a stress
on interpersonal relations and situations in which controlled
experiments could be introduced. Finally, it is also symp-
tomatic of the disillusionment of many American sociologists
with the panaceas of socialism, which previously had provided
a tacit ideological justification for dealing with larger social
issues.[3]

[2] See Edward A. Shils, "The Study of the Primary Group," in Lerner
and Lasswell, *The Policy Sciences* (Stanford: Stanford University Press,
1951). This excellent article places the research on small groups in historical
perspective.

[3] See Lewis Coser, "The Functions of Small Group Research," *Social
Problems*, Vol. 3, No. 1, July 1955. The author suggests, in the context of
a study of "the sociology of knowledge," that the current vogue of small
group studies is at least partly to be understood as a response to the pressure
on younger scholars to publish in order to facilitate promotion. In support
of this he states that such research can be easily summarized in small, pub-
lishable articles; is experimental and usually entails the use of some statistical techniques; is easily carried out by using as subjects the members of
"captive" groups such as students, members of the armed forces, prisoners
or Boy Scouts; and is unlikely to offend the senior members of academic
departments by invading their areas of vested interest, as it is a comparatively
new field. Professor Coser does not disguise his hostility to this type of
research, but claims that his analysis of the motivation behind such research
has no relevance for its validity. We shall return to this problem in the
final chapter.

American Critique of Theory of Mass Society:

The sociological emphasis on the primary group has not been confined to research on mass communications. Katz in his historical summary[4] cites the Hawthorne studies,[5] which illustrated the importance of the primary group in industry; the studies in *The American Soldier*[6] of primary groups in the military context; and the Yankee City[7] studies, which served to emphasize the importance of cliques in the social structure of an urban community. In tracing the antecedents of the present-day interest in small group research among social psychologists and sociologists,[8] Shils cites three main influences: the "human relations" studies in industrial sociology carried on by Elton Mayo and his associates; the work of J. L. Moreno in sociometry—the mapping of patterns of attraction and repulsion in small groups; and the "group dynamics" research of Kurt Lewin. Now for our purposes, the first of these is far more important than the last two; the first is an example of sociological inquiry into the actual workings of "mass society" and the problem of the influence of interpersonal ties, whereas the last two are purely psychological— that is, they are concerned with the processes of perception and judgment in individuals, and the extent to which these processes are influenced by group contexts.

Most of these studies were carried on during the middle 1930's. A powerful impetus for research on small groups came from the Hawthorne project, a now-famous experiment in which sociologists unwittingly created primary-group ties among a special group of workers under observation in a factory. Variations in lighting and work tempo, being tested for their effects on production, seemed to have no effects

[4] Elihu Katz and Paul Lazarsfeld, *Personal Influence* (Glencoe: Free Press, 1955), Section I, Part II. Professor Katz acknowledges his indebtedness to the article by Shils, above.

[5] O. F. J. Roethlisberger and W. J. Dickson, *Management and the Worker* (Cambridge: Harvard University Press, 1939).

[6] Samuel A. Stouffer, et al., *The American Soldier* (Princeton: Princeton University Press, 1949), Vol. II.

[7] W. Lloyd Warner and Paul S. Lunt, *The Social Life of a Modern Community* (New Haven: Yale University Press, 1941), Vol. I.

[8] *Op. cit.*, n. 52.

whatever on a production curve which kept rising. It was not until afterwards that the researchers were able to determine what had happened. The special attention given these workers in the course of the experiment had created a group-feeling and mutual identification which ultimately "ruined" the original experiment by introducing an intervening variable. This "discovery" ultimately gave rise to a whole school of industrial sociology, which stressed the importance of primary-group satisfactions in the work process, and made the industrial sociologist or psychologist a fixture in every "modern" factory. This school has been roundly criticized for their allegedly pro-management bias; the workers, it is argued, are being manipulated by the human relations technicians, solely in the interests of increased production.[9] Whether this is true or not, sociologists no longer think in terms of individual, isolated, "alienated" workers, but concentrate on the kinds of inter-action among working groups and the social context of the work itself.

Research in the field of mass communications, however, provided the main context for the questioning of the theory of mass society. Professor Raymond Bauer, in a forthcoming paper,[10] suggests that three major premises of the theory of mass society have been questioned by the results of American mass communications research. Somewhat amplified and re-stated, these are: 1. Modern mass society has resulted in a breakdown of the primary groups, so that informal com-munications play a relatively minor role in the reception of the mass media. 2. The audience for mass communications is an atomized one, consisting of individuals from different

[9] Cf. Reinhard Bendix and Lloyd Fisher, "The Perspectives of Elton Mayo," *Review of Economics and Statistics*, 31, 1949, pp. 312-319, and the interesting discussion of this problem in Daniel Bell, *Work and Its Dis-contents* (Boston: Beacon, 1956).

[10] Raymond Bauer and Alice H. Bauer, "American Society and the Mass Media of Communication," *Journal of Social Issues*, 1961 (forthcoming). My own views and those of the authors developed independently but converge at several important points. I am grateful to the authors for allowing me to read their suggestive paper.

backgrounds who are uprooted, isolated, anonymous and detached. 3. The mass media themselves are omnipotent; they can influence attitudes and behavior at will, and whoever controls the mass media can manipulate the isolated individuals in the mass with considerable ease. In Bauer's terms, "content and effect may be equated."

Now points (1) and (2) are really so closely related as to constitute a single idea—the absence of significant primary groups and the isolation of the individual—which (3) makes him an easy target for manipulation by the mass media.

These ideas were subjected to criticism by researchers and theorists, beginning around 1940. It was in that year that a study of the 1940 election campaign, published in 1948, did so much to question the imagery of the theorists of mass society.[11] The researchers conducted a careful panel study in which the opinions of a large sample of residents in Erie County, Ohio, were followed over several months. The mass media at this time were generally hostile to Roosevelt. The results of the study were relevant for both points discussed above. Family members tended to vote in the same way, and those who made up their minds earlier in the campaign tended to be followed by those who were still uncertain. Thus there was a kind of "bandwagon effect" observed, but on the family rather than on the national level. After the gathering of additional data, this study yielded another hypothesis concerning the flow of mass communications. The communications process was now visualized as having two phases; those people who had actually changed their voting intentions had not done so as a result of the influence of the newspapers or the radio, but because of personal contacts. Thus the small group was viewed as intervening between the mass media and the individual-in-the-mass, modifying the effects of the former. American sociologists became sensitized to the social context of communications behavior, whereas before, the formulations

[11] Paul F. Lazarsfeld, Bernard Berelson and Hazel Gaudet, *The People's Choice* (New York: Columbia University Press, 1948).

of Park,[12] Blumer[13] and Wirth[14] had retained elements of the European theory of mass society, by their insistence on the isolation, anonymity and detachment of the individual, the lack of a social context, and the breakdown of the primary groups, as well as the power of the mass media in molding opinion.

A further refinement was introduced by Merton in his study of opinion leaders.[15] The people in a small community were observed with an eye to determining who were the "influentials," the ones to whom others looked for signals. The opinion leader was viewed as mediating between the mass media and the individual-in-the-mass. These opinion leaders tended to sift and filter the available mass media material, and pass judgment on how these were to be interpreted. Thus the media often did not act directly on the individual-in-the-mass, but were judged and censored, interpreted and evaluated by the opinion leader within the group context. Merton differentiated two groups of opinion leaders

[12] See Chapter 3. In Park's view the mass media functioned to reestablish the *Gemeinschaft.* Of the newspaper, he wrote: "The motive, conscious or unconscious, of the writers and of the press in all this is to reproduce, as far as possible, in the city the conditions of life in the village. In the village everyone knew everyone else. Everyone called everyone by his first name. The village was democratic. We are a nation of villagers. Our institutions are fundamentally village institutions. In the village, gossip and public opinion were the main sources of social control. . . . It is evident that a newspaper cannot do for a community of one million inhabitants what the village did spontaneously for itself through the medium of gossip and personal contact. Nevertheless the efforts of the newspaper to achieve this impossible result are an interesting chapter in the history of politics as well as of the press." R. E. Park, "The Natural History of the Newspaper," in E. C. Hughes (ed.), *Society* (Glencoe: Free Press, 1955), pp. 93-94.

[13] Blumer, *op. cit.,* 1935, 1939.

[14] Louis Wirth, "Consensus and Mass Communications," *American Sociological Review,* Vol. 13, Feb. 1948, pp. 1-14. Professor Wirth was an important member of the Chicago school, who perpetuated elements of the European theory of mass society in his concept of consensus and the mass. He was a student of Park's and was also very much influenced by Karl Mannheim.

[15] Robert K. Merton, "Patterns of Influence: A Study of Interpersonal Influence and of Communications Behavior in a Social Community," in Lazarsfeld and Stanton (eds.), *Communications Research, 1948-1949* (New York: Harper, 1949).

within the community under study: the "local" and the "cosmopolitan." The local opinion leaders were oriented toward the small-town community, would not think of living anywhere else, and were less interested in the larger world. The cosmopolitan opinion leaders reported that they had often thought of leaving the local community, and that they could live in another town if necessary. The cosmopolitans had lived elsewhere previously, while the locals tended to be natives of the town who had not lived away from home except for a brief time.

Both of these groups were influential in the community, but the character of their communication with their fellow townspeople varied considerably. The locals tended to be more gregarious—joining organizations such as secret societies, fraternal organizations, local service clubs, in order to make more contacts—and active in local politics that depended on a wide base of local support. The cosmopolitans were not members of as many groups as the locals; they stressed the importance of the qualities of the people they knew rather than sheer numbers. The range of their personal relations was limited to such areas as professional societies, where special skills and knowledge were important. Their public positions also stressed special knowledge and skill, rather than reflecting involvement in such a broad local base of patronage and friendship as the political network of the locals. Thus the cosmopolitans were often found on the Board of Education, Housing Committee, Board of Health, etc. Further, the locals were asked about many more different kinds of situations than the cosmopolitans; the latter were approached as sources of specialized information, while the locals were approached as friendly individuals who could be helpful without generating status anxieties. From this study it also appears that influence is stratified, and that there are levels of influential and influenced people, each constituting a kind of reference group. It is also characterized by hierarchy, in that those at the middle level of influence look up toward those at the top.

This suggestive study indicated that there were elements in the process of mass communications which had not been adequately treated before. Subsequent studies tried to assess the theoretical significance of these new developments and also to carry on further research. David Riesman's studies of popular culture indicated the importance of the teen-age peer group in the "consumption" of the mass media, and emphasized the process of "taste-exchange" by virtue of which status was established within the group. The implications here were that, contrary to the imagery of the theory of mass society, most people attended to the mass media within some kind of group context, and for the adolescent in particular, the family group and the peer group assumed great importance.[16]

These developments rendered the concept of the "reference group" important in communications research.[17] Until 1953, however, there was no explicit and systematic attempt to confront Blumer's theory of mass behavior with this new evidence and try to assess the theory. This was achieved in an article by Eliot Friedson.[18] Blumer's theory was compared with the evidence from such previously cited sources as Lazarsfeld, Riley and Flowerman, and Merton. Friedson pointed out that even Lazarsfeld used the idea of "mass media" in the sense of a message reaching all individuals and

[16] I have explored the implications of Riesman's work for Blumer's conception of mass behavior in an unpublished paper, "The Concept of the Mass," Spring 1951.

[17] See Matilda W. Riley and Samuel H. Flowerman, "Group Relations as a Variable in Communications Research," *American Sociological Review*, Vol. 16, April 1951. Members and non-members of peer-groups are there referred to as "high" and "low" communicators, with verbal interaction used as an index of group integration. Cf. M. W. Riley and J. W. Riley, "A Sociological Approach to Communications Research," *Public Opinion Quarterly*, Vol. 15, 1951, pp. 445-460.

[18] Eliot Friedson, "Communications Research and the Concept of the Mass," *American Sociological Review*, Vol. 18, pp. 313-317. Reprinted in W. Schramm (ed.) *Process and Effects of Mass Communication* (Urbana: University of Illinois, 1955).

groups of the population uniformly.[19] He then showed that such a conception of the mass, particularly Blumer's formulation, is inadequate for the description of the audience of mass communications, and cited the view of Riley and Flowerman: "Any given person in the audience reacts not merely as an isolated personality but also as a member of the various groups to which he belongs and with which he communicates."[20]

Friedson cites the evidence of recent research to the effect that most people go to the movies in the company of another person rather than alone,[21] and that family rather than solitary listening and watching are characteristic of radio and television audiences.[22] He also notes Merton's "discovery" of the opinion-leader, and studio-sponsored research indicating the importance of the transmission of opinions from one person to another in the process of "selection" of a movie. This selection process was previously visualized by theorists like Blumer within a context of individual isolation. Rather than serving to undermine the local culture, as Blumer indicated, the evidence points to the fact that mass communications have been absorbed into the social life of the local culture. The audience, although made up of individuals, is engaged in a selection process which is guided by the social groups of which these individuals are members. The act of selection itself tends to become habitual rather than self-conscious, and research indi-

[19] P. F. Lazarsfeld and P. L. Kendall, "The Communications Behavior of the Average American," in W. Schramm (ed.), *Mass Communications* (Urbana: University of Illinois Press, 1949), p. 399. "The term 'mass,' then is truly applicable to the medium of radio, for it more than the other media, reaches all groups of the population uniformly."

[20] *Op. cit.*, p. 171.

[21] Leo A. Handel, *Hollywood Looks at Its Audience* (Urbana: University of Illinois Press, 1950), pp. 113-114. The author was the first full-time research director employed by a major Hollywood studio. He carried out careful audience studies and contributed a valuable critique of previous studio research.

[22] A. L. Eisenberg, *Children and Radio Programs* (New York: Columbia University Press, 1936), p. 194; and E. E. Maccoby, "Television: Its Impact on School Children," *Public Opinion Quarterly*, Vol. 15, 1951, p. 425. These studies, however, are all concerned with children and adolescents rather than adults.

cates that only about 21 per cent of the movie audience showed any conscious effort to select a particular movie, rather than going to the local theater on Saturday night as a matter of habit.[23]

"Much audience behavior, then, takes place in a complex network of local social activity. Certain times of day, certain days, certain sessions, are the socially appropriate times for engaging in particular activities connected with the various mass media. The individual is frequently accompanied by others of his social group when he is engaged in these activities. The individual participates in an interpersonal grid of spectators who discuss the meaning of past experience with mass communications and the anticipated significance of future experience. Certain theaters, programs and newspapers tend to form focal points for his activity on certain occasions no matter what the content might actually be."[24]

But this new perspective on the context of mass communications also has important implications for the idea of manipulation in the theory of mass society. If the intervening primary groups are in fact as powerful and influential as research indicates, there is no guarantee that the media can in fact manipulate the "masses" so easily, or that from a knowledge of the contents of a communication one can infer the effects. The evidence is quite to the contrary; Joseph T. Klapper, in an early paper, pointed out that it is the group context of mass communications which prevents the easy inference of effects on the basis of content.[25] Friedson declares that "on the basis of this material on the experience and behavior of members of the audience, it is possible to conclude that the audience, from the point of view of its members, at least, is *not* anonymous, heterogenous, unorganized and spatially separated. The individual member of the audience frequently does not

[23] Handel, *op. cit.*, p. 69.
[24] Friedson, *op. cit.*, p. 385 (Schramm).
[25] Joseph T. Klapper, "The Effects of the Mass Media" (New York: Bureau of Applied Social Research, Columbia University, 1949), Section I-15, p. 6. Cited by Friedson, *supra*.

manifest the selective activity characteristic of the mass, and when such selection has been observed to occur it appeared to arise out of the stimulation of organized social processes rather than merely the individual's personal interests. Given this, it is possible to conclude that the concept of the mass is not accurately applicable to the audience."[26]

The most recent work representing continuity in this field of inquiry is *Personal Influence*.[27] This study represents an effort to confirm the hypotheses suggested and partially confirmed in *The People's Choice* (1948) and in Merton's work on the role of the opinion leader in mass communication. Decatur, Illinois, was selected for study after an exhaustive inquiry to determine which small city was most typical in terms of average characteristics available in quantified form in census materials. An attempt to locate opinion leaders was made and following this, an effort to determine the relative influence of the mass media versus personal contacts in four specific areas of decision-making. These areas were daily household marketing; fashion in women's clothes, cosmetics and beauty aids; public affairs under discussion at the time; and movie attendance. Previous studies had indicated that each social stratum generated its own opinion leaders—the individuals who were most likely to influence other people in their social environment. These individuals were more likely to expose themselves to mass communications especially suited to their educational level and interests. The study in Decatur was an attempt to test this theory. The sample was composed of a cross-section of women; each respondent was asked whether she had recently made a change or reached a decision in any of these four areas. If she had, she was asked a large number of questions in an effort to find out which media and/or people had influenced her. Through another procedure, there was an effort to identify the opinion leaders, those who would be most likely to be singled out for advice

[26] Friedson, *op. cit.*, pp. 385-386.
[27] Katz and Lazarsfeld, *op. cit.*

within their social stratum. The results tended in general to confirm the authors' hypothesis concerning the existence of horizontal opinion leadership and the importance of personal influence.[28]

The authors mention two results of current small group research which they consider of particular relevance.

(1) Ostensibly private opinions and attitudes are often generated and/or reinforced in small intimate groups of family, friends, and co-workers. Opinions are more stable if they are shared by a group, and, under pressure of a "campaign," people are more likely to change opinions jointly than individually.

(2) Families, friendships, work-groups and the like are interpersonal communications networks through which influences flow in patterned ways. The leader is a strategic element in the formation of group opinions; he is more aware of what the several members think; he mediates between them; and he represents something like the "typical" group mind.[29]

It is clear that the authors regard these general hypotheses as confirmed by their study. They admit, however, that there is another aspect of the communications picture; one which probably would be stressed by a theorist of mass society. Speaking of the plan of the book, they say: "Originally, a third section was contemplated; it should at least be mentioned so that the reader can see the problem of personal influence in its total context. The way in which people influence each other is not only affected by the primary groups within which they live; it is co-determined by the broad institutional setting of the American scene."[30]

Interview materials which pertained to such influences, however, were not included in the study. They were declared to

[28] The last is discussed under the title of "the two-step flow" of influence, a metaphor designed to emphasize the fact that the flow moves from the mass media to the opinion leaders and *then* to the individuals-in-the-mass, within their social contexts. See Part ii, Ch. 15.

[29] *Ibid.*, pp. 8-9.

[30] *Ibid.*, p. 9.

be "too sketchy" for inclusion; they did not lend themselves to quantification and arrangement into tables. The authors did not want to go beyond the point at which they could still show that their generalizations were empirically verifiable. In this respect they were prisoners of their methodology, and represent the contraction of the field of sociology cited by Wirth, the emphasis on verifiability and the tendency to deal with theories of the "middle-range." The theorist of mass society would no doubt find their study deficient in this respect; that they miss the role of the larger institutional context and the power of the mass media themselves. For do not the mass media still influence the opinion leaders, and thus are not the opinion leaders being manipulated? We will return to this problem in Chapter Six. But this brings us back to the question of manipulation. We have mentioned this as the third point on which the theory of mass society is being questioned by research in mass communications. For that theory insists that a consequence of the isolation of the individuals in the mass is that they are all the more easily manipulated by the mass media, particularly in the hands of a clever demagogue. The Marxist variation of the theory of mass society has it that the mass media are molding the minds of the people, at the same time providing them with a narcotic in the form of popular culture, which prevents them from realizing their common interests and joining together for the overthrow of the exploiters. As Shils has correctly noted,[31] many contemporary critiques of this type are free from the aridities of Marxist dogmatics while at the same time originating in a transmuted Marxism in which "capitalism" as the villain of the drama has been replaced by "mass culture."

Now to the extent that mass communications research has revealed the existence and the importance of intermediary groups between the media and the "masses," it has also undermined this concept of manipulatability as following from the atomization and isolation of the individuals who compose the

[31] See *infra*, Chapter Six, note 3.

mass. So that evidence which contradicts the one image will also contradict the other. The study of the 1940 presidential election, for example, also indicated that the mass media were not, in fact, omnipotent, since the press and the radio were predominantly opposed to Roosevelt. During the same period in which the "rediscovery of the primary group" took place—that is, roughly from the middle 1930's—a similar movement was under way with respect to the limits of the effectiveness of the mass media for persuasion and manipulation. Where previously there had been a widespread belief in the omnipotence of the media, now several studies and even some "armchair" research indicated that this was misleading. From the field of fashion came evidence that some styles could not be ballyhooed into popularity, but ended in financial failure and loss of tens of thousands of dollars by "the manipulators." Motion pictures, representing a considerable investment on the part of the producers, sometimes did not elicit a sufficient response on the part of the public to cover costs. Some movies made large profits, while others, although widely advertised and promoted, failed at the box-office. Few sociologists troubled to ask why some movies did not attract audiences while others were financially successful.[32]

Information campaigns, subjected to checks by survey analysis, were revealed to be quite ineffective in certain circumstances. One case, cited by Bauer, involved a survey conducted during the last war to determine why people bought war bonds. Most of the people surveyed in April, 1943, declared that they bought war bonds in order to help finance the war. Against 65 per cent who answered in this way, 14 per cent said that they bought war bonds in order to prevent inflation. A large-scale advertising campaign was mounted during the next few years, with the emphasis on the buying of war bonds to prevent inflation. But in June, 1945, the results of a re-survey showed that 68 per cent of the people thought bonds

---

[32] With the exception of Handel, *op. cit.*, and David Riesman, "Movies and Audiences," *Individualism Reconsidered, op. cit.*

should be bought to help finance the war, and 14 per cent thought they should be bought to aid in preventing inflation.[33]

During the war itself there were many studies carried out by the research branch of the Information and Education Division of the War Department.[34] These studies, mostly experiments concerning changes in attitudes resulting from exposure to different kinds of communications media, revealed that such communications have a wide variety of effects, and that the group context is an important factor in the process. Thus they too contributed to a shift in the image of the mass media as capable of easy manipulation of audiences.

The best-known and most instructive example of the failure of an information campaign occurred after the war in Cincinnati, Ohio. In September, 1947, three organizations in that city undertook a large-scale information campaign designed to present facts about the United Nations and to demonstrate, as they put it, "how a community may become so intelligently informed on world affairs as to be a dynamic force in the creation of an ordered and eventually a peaceful world." There is no question that the flow of information on the subject increased during the six months of the campaign.

"To mention only a few of the activities: 12,868 people were reached through the P.T.A.'s which devoted programs to the topic of world understanding. Every school child was given literature on the United Nations to take home; the schoolteachers kept the subject constantly before their pupils and were themselves supplied with instructions and materials at teachers' mass meetings. Fourteen thousand children in the Weekday Church Schools held a World Community Day program; 150 leaders in the Cincinnati Council of Church Women took training courses in the arranging of United Nations programs; 10,000 members of the Catholic P.T.A.

[33] Mason Haire, *Psychology in Management* (New York: McGraw-Hill, 1956), p. 81, cited by Bauer, *op. cit.*

[34] See Carl I. Hovland, Arthur A. Lumsdaine and Fred D. Sheffield, *Experiments in Mass Communications* (Princeton: Princeton University Press, 1949), cited by Bauer, *op. cit.*

were exhorted by their archbishop to support the United Nations; and a group of club women united in sending 1,000 letters and 1,350 telegrams pledging their support to the American delegation to the United Nations. The radio stations broadcast facts about the United Nations, one of them scheduling spot programs 150 times a week. The newspapers played up United Nations news and information throughout the six months. In the last three months 225 meetings were served with literature and special speakers. In all, 59,588 pieces of literature were distributed and 2,800 clubs were reached by speakers supplied by a speakers' bureau and by circular, hundreds of documentary films were shown, and the slogan 'Peace Begins with the United Nations—The United Nations Begins With You' was exhibited everywhere, in every imaginable form—blotters, matchbooks, streetcar cards, etc. The objective was to reach in one way or another every adult among the 1,155,703 residents of Cincinnati's retail trading zone."[35]

The National Opinion Research Council, working with these organizations, made a before-and-after study to determine the effectiveness of the campaign. The results of this study are limited, as they estimate only the short-run rather than the long-run effects. Yet they indicate that most scores remained about the same after the campaign as they had been before; some improved, and some were less favorable. The researchers concluded that the campaign had succeeded in reaching precisely those people who were already convinced of the value of the United Nations, and had not reached those who were simply uninterested or who had negative attitudes. The researchers' view is that people will pay attention to publicity which is congenial to their already existing attitudes. This phenomenon, observed by many students of the communications process, has been dubbed "self-selection."[36]

[35] Shirley A. Star and Helen MacGill Hughes, "Report on an Educational Campaign: The Cincinnati Plan for the United Nations," *American Journal of Sociology*, Vol. 55, No. 4, January 1950, p. 390.

[36] Cf. Herbert H. Hyman and Paul B. Sheatsley, "Some Reasons Why

American Critique of Theory of Mass Society:

Political scientists in particular have been prone to assume the omnipotence of the mass media in the hands of a totalitarian regime, which could proceed to make their citizens believe anything. This Orwellian vision has been seriously impaired by communications research on the reaction to government information sources even under conditions of totalitarian rule.[37] The situation of a communications "monopoly" is indeed one in which it is possible to exercise considerable control over the news itself, not to speak of the image of the world which is entertained by the citizen. Yet recent history has provided examples of some "boomerangs" in mass communications, perhaps the most important being the public reaction in the Soviet Union and the satellite countries of Eastern Europe to the release of Khrushchev's denunciation of Stalin.

The results of this research in mass communications, however, should not be considered completely unambiguous. I will try to show, in succeeding pages, the extent to which the results may be subjected to alternative interpretations. One final irony remains, however, in the critique of the theory of mass society by American students of mass communication. These sociologists, ostensibly liberals, have focused on an aspect of American life which, by implication, tends to contradict the individualistic and rationalistic premises which form part of the basis of the liberal tradition. On the one hand, their analyses of decision-making, voting, and the formation

---

Information Campaigns Fail," *Public Opinion Quarterly*, Fall 1947, pp. 412-423.

[37] For example, cf. Riesman, *op. cit.*, and A. Inkeles, *Public Opinion in Soviet Russia* (Cambridge: Harvard University Press, 1950). When, as in Communist China, the mass media messages are combined with small group discussion, writing of critical autobiographies, public self-criticism and confession, however, their impact is considerably enhanced. See William Stevenson, *The Yellow Wind* (Boston: Houghton Mifflin, 1959).

of opinion do indicate that the mass media of communication are not as powerful as they were once thought to be. On the other hand, their studies of the communication process all emphasize the extent to which such decision-making, even in the political sphere, is based on non-rational factors such as the influence of peer groups and reference groups. They have contributed a new image of the mass audience which is perhaps scarcely more flattering than that of the European theorists of mass society. It is a picture which shows individuals whose ostensibly private, rational opinions are being molded by the reference groups and opinion leaders who, at the same time, must at least partially reflect their values.

It is instructive and revealing that because of the ahistorical tradition of American sociology, there was no attempt to trace the concept of the mass—for example, in Blumer's formulation—back to its European setting. Possibly the belief that they employed value-free categories enabled American sociologists to overlook the political implications of this whole problem. It must also be said that until recently there was no interest in comparative studies to test these "discoveries" about mass communications audiences in other cultural settings than the American. The structure of American sociology itself is a part of the explanation; the absolute sense of the American social structure and the middle-class standard of life which characterized the perspective of so many American sociologists tended to discourage comparative studies of this type. Such studies were left to American anthropologists, who, because of the historical circumstances of a tradition of research in primitive cultures, tended until recently to ignore the materials offered by modern, industrialized societies.

I mention this because of what, in looking back, seems to have been a lack of awareness on the part of the communications researchers that they were dealing with the European theory of mass society in their revision of the concept of the mass communications audience. If they were not ideologically innocent, or perhaps only ideologically unconscious, there is still no evidence of it in their writings on this subject. Perhaps it is the legitimate function of the intellectual historian, the historian of sociology itself, to try to assess the significance of such movements of thought.

From a strictly sociological standpoint, it must be noted that this research is open to several different interpretations, so far as its relation to the theory of mass society is concerned. I will list a few:

1. It is possible that the theory of mass society was a useful one in the late 19th century, to help explain the conditions brought about under a more fully developed capitalism-industrialism. Thus the new facts uncovered by the mass communications researchers would be relevant to a later phase.

The mass communications researchers would probably reply that the material they have uncovered, particularly that relating to the influence of primary groups, was precisely that which would be ignored by a social scientist intent on using the framework provided by the theory of mass society. In fact, they would claim that the widespread acceptance of this theory had led to the systematic neglect of the influence of small groups in the mass communications process and in social life generally.

2. The data uncovered by the mass communications researchers is relevant only for America and for American society. For Europe the theory of mass society still holds true, and provides the best tool for understanding and explanation.

This is an attractive idea, because it involves a concept of American exceptionalism. Unfortunately I knew of no comparative studies extant which could demonstrate conclusively that the same process is at work in European as in American mass communications,[38] but research on the Near and Middle

---

[38] But cf. Alfred Vierkandt, *Kleine Gesellschaftslehre* (Stuttgart: F. Enke,

East indicates that many of the same processes observed by the American researchers are important in mass communications in those areas.[39]

3. The fact that opinion leaders and small groups are mediating between the media and "the mass" does not change the true picture: the mass media are still manipulating the opinion leaders.

This is of course the response of the theorists of mass society. They wish to continue the imagery of the omnipotent mass media. But if the revelations of the mass communications researchers are accurate, what sense does it make to speak of direct "manipulation" by the mass media? But the argument of these theorists is built on such ambiguity.

4. The mass communications research does not change the picture at all. The theory of mass society is still "essentially" true. The fact that opinion leaders and small groups are mediating between the mass media and the individuals-in-the-mass does not have an effect on the quality of the experience of those individuals. They are still "essentially" alienated: from each other, and from themselves.

This is of course the theorist of mass society again. His argument would be as follows: the fact that five or six people are watching a television program together and are discussing it afterwards does not mean that they are interacting "significantly." Their interaction may be on a very shallow level, or they may not "really" be interacting at all. The television audience here would just be another example of the segmentalization of the self stressed by many sociologists; each person would be presenting only a small part of himself for participa-

---

1948); and P. Hofstadter, *Dynamiek der Gruppen: Critic der Massenpsychologie* (Hamburg: Rowohlt, 1956).

[39] For example, Daniel Lerner (ed.), *The Passing of Traditional Society* (Glencoe: Free Press, 1958); J. Mayone Stycos, "Patterns of Communication in a Rural Greek Village," *Public Opinion Quarterly*, Vol. 16, No. 4, Spring 1952, pp. 59-70. Cf. also Bruce L. Smith, "Communications Research in Non-Industrial Countries," in Schramm (ed.), *op. cit.*, pp. 170-79; and United States Information Service, "Prestige, Personal Influence, and Opinion," *Ibid.*, p. 404ff.

tion in this "interaction." The whole person is never involved. This is the meaning of alienation from self and others: one treats others as objects, and ends by treating oneself as an object. This theme has been stressed by Fromm, Buber and the Existentialists.

There runs through this whole argument a tacit acceptance of the ancient distinction between appearance and reality. Thus the individuals who go to the movies together or watch television are not really interacting, they only *appear* to be doing so. Social scientists, however, work on the level of appearances. They are committed to the study of the phenomenal rather than the noumenal world. They hold that the noumenal realm is beyond the reach of science, but the argument of the theorists of mass society, presented as "science," denies this. It is not only in social and political philosophy that these theorists are distinguished by their elitism. Their epistemology is also involved: they must postulate an elite of knowers who can break through the veil of appearances and penetrate to "essential" reality. Thus it is ironic that these theorists should present their argument as "scientific." They are romantics who are not satisfied with the limits of scientific empiricism.

Science cannot measure the quality of an experience. There exists no metric unit by virtue of which this could be effected. An argument about the "essential quality"of an experience is not a scientific one; it is an aesthetic or philosophical one. It must rest on extra-scientific judgments. Yet the Golden Age which many mass society theorists look back upon, or forward to, as the antithesis of "modern alienation," is held to be a superior one in precisely those terms. No sensitive person could deny that the modern era has been distinguished by a peculiar range of horrors. Yet this is not seen the better by projecting the image of a non-existent medieval synthesis or future realm of freedom, in which men were or will be possessed of "true autonomy," or "authenticity," or some of the other words used to describe their condition in that happy time. Men in those past days had other troubles, as contemporary historians have increasingly become aware. Our problems are different from many of theirs, for we have solved some of those which beset them most cruelly. In the wake of the solutions came new problems. Contemporary sociological pessimism suggests that this might be true of future utopias as well.

The truth of the matter is that the results of all this American research on the effects of the mass media of communication have had very little effect on the theory of mass society. It should be clear by now that the chief reason for this is that the theory is not a scientific one, nor even one based exclusively on solid historical research. It is a world-perspective, an ideology which has its source in some movements of thought of the 19th century which we have discussed above. As such, there is no way in which it could be "proven" wrong. It is an attitude on the part of specific social theorists and some sociologists. It is not based entirely on scientific evidence. Where a piece of data or evidence is ambiguous, it is always "interpreted" by theorists of mass society as supporting that theory. There is little taste for ambiguity among these theorists.[40]

Perhaps an example will make this more clear. When learning to do sociological field work I was obliged to obtain a number of interviews among apartment-dwellers in a census tract on the south side of Chicago. Part of the interview assignment was to obtain a genealogy of the respondents. There was an interesting difference between the genealogies of an upper-middle class couple who had lived in a fashionable apartment in the city for a long time, and those of a lower-middle class couple living in a basement, who had just come to Chicago from a farm near Niles, Michigan. The first couple could only go back one and at most two generations in their genealogical recollection, and there were many relations whom they could not remember; they listed a dozen people. The farm couple between them contributed a family

[40] This is noted by Bauer in his forthcoming paper, *op. cit.*, Ch. 3, p. 18ff.

tree showing the precise relationship to them of some 120 different persons.

The theorist of mass society would interpret this undeniably "empirical" evidence as indicating the loss of social ties, the increasing alienation of urban life, the lack of a feeling of community, the destruction of the extended family, a symbol of social disorganization. The liberal sociologist would interpret the *same* data as indicating the new potentialities for a creative and individualistic life without the tyranny of the provincial small town and the Victorian family. He would stress the new opportunities for an independent life available in the city, greater freedom for personal development, without the control of a family which in the past could operate as an autocracy or oligarchy demanding subservience to its whims and desires. He would stress the element of choice— the existence of alternatives—in the choice of friends and associates, where before there was no choice but association dictated by custom and circumstance.

I do not see how one could say whether either of these views was "true"; they are not the kinds of propositions which can be termed "true" or "false." They are world-perspectives, not scientific hypotheses. The theorist of mass society prefers to see through a glass darkly. The blend of romanticism, existentialism, Marxism and psychoanalysis which forms the basis of his world-perspective give him a certain shadowy picture. It is, like all world-perspectives, both restrictive and facilitative. It prevents him from seeing some things and allows him to see others. But it is not "based on science." There is no magic key which will allow us to throw open the doors of a social philosophy founded on pure science. David Hume pointed this out some time ago, but later German and French philosophers did not find this a useful bit of intelligence. Indeed, they found it quite intolerable, and, allowing for a proper period of incubation during the 19th century, we may see the results in the theory of mass society.

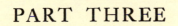

PART THREE

CHAPTER SIX

MASS SOCIETY, MASS CULTURE, AND TOTALITARIANISM

IN Chapter Two, a *précis* of the theory of mass society was offered which stressed the elitism of these theorists, whether of the Left or the Right: their preference for a hierarchically-ordered society; their hostility to individualist liberalism; stress on the costs of social mobility, and on the infiltration of the cultural minorities; and the extra-scientific character of some of their judgments. In returning to the mass society theorists at this point, I wish to review some aspects of the imputed relation between mass culture and totalitarianism often stressed by members of this school, with special emphasis on the psychology of the mass man.

It is in the discussion of that aspect of the theory of mass society which is expressed as a concern over "mass culture" that the ideological elements of the theory are enunciated most clearly. It is difficult to separate those aspects of the mass society theory which are specifically cultural from those which are political; this part of the theory culminates in both a cultural critique and a political sociology. The best examples of the critique of mass culture are provided by European sociologists and social theorists, many of whom are now or were until recently resident in the United States. They are European *émigrés* who have brought to bear on this question, not surprisingly, a particularly European outlook.[1] They have made some converts among American sociologists.[2] The views

[1] Cf. Leo Lowenthal, "Historical Perspectives of Popular Culture," in B. Rosenberg and D. M. White (eds.), *Mass Culture* (Glencoe: Free Press, 1956), pp. 46-58; Gunther Anders, "The Phantom World of TV," *ibid.*, pp. 358-367; T. W. Adorno, "Television and the Patterns of Mass Culture," *ibid.*, pp. 474-488; and Max Horkheimer, "Art and Mass Culture," *Studies in Philosophy and Social Science*, Vol. 9, 1941; Erich Fromm, *Escape From Freedom* (New York: Rinehart, 1948).

[2] Cf. Bernard Rosenberg, "Mass Culture in America," in Rosenberg and White, *op. cit.*, pp. 3-12; Dwight MacDonald, "A Theory of Mass Culture,"

of these theorists arise out of a context completely different from the criticisms of Ortega or T. S. Eliot. These earlier critics of culture under liberal democracy developed an anti-bourgeois view similar to some that we have analyzed in 19th-century thought. The European critics of mass society, however, far from finding their point of departure on the Right, have intellectual roots in the politics of the Left.[3] It may seem astonishing that the idea of mass culture—or as its liberal defenders term it, popular culture—should be attacked by thinkers influenced by the egalitarian tradition of Marxism. Mass culture is, after all, the culture of "the masses." But perhaps this is because, as many have observed, Marxism contains within it the seeds of an elitist philosophy, not an egalitarian one. Here again, the lines are drawn in such a way that the Left and the Right are united against the liberal-individualism of the center. By a curious alchemy of politics, the Marxist framework, now employed without the orthodox terminology, became the theoretical basis for an attack on the culture of "the masses" under capitalism.

But according to these critics, it is no longer capitalism which is the sole cause of the evils which beset the man of today. It is modern industrial society, which has solved some

ibid., pp. 59-73; Irving Howe, "Notes on Mass Culture," *ibid.,* pp. 496-503; and C. Wright Mills, *The Power Elite* (New York: Oxford University Press, 1956), Ch. 13.

[3] Cf. the documentation presented in Edward Shils, "Daydreams and Nightmares: Reflections on the Criticism of Mass Culture," *The Sewanee Review,* Vol. 65, No. 4, October-December 1957, pp. 587-608, especially p. 589. The analysis presented by Shils is similar to the one presented here in previous chapters, to the extent that he finds the origins of the theory of mass society in a 19th century anti-liberal tradition, which ranges from French conservatism to German sociological romanticism and Marxism. Shils regards the critical interpretation of mass culture as "a product of disappointed political prejudices, vague aspirations for an unattainable ideal, resentment against American society, and at bottom, romanticism dressed up in the language of sociology, psychoanalysis and existentialism" (p. 596). Though I agree with the Shils' argument in the main, and the extent of my dependence on his admirable critical article will become obvious in the following pages, it should also become clear that I regard his judgment of the mass society theorists to be somewhat harsh.

of the older problems of poverty and hard physical labor, but created new problems in the form of boredom, vulgarity, and "mass taste." The masses, previously idealized by thinkers like Marx, Engels and Trotsky, had not achieved the cultural heights which these thinkers had declared would follow upon the advent of a reorganized industrial society. The theorists of mass society, far from idealizing the masses, now see their adaptation to industrial society as a waste of time in the cultural slums, the underworld of the movies, comics, popular songs, pulp magazines, television violence and cheap journalism. The masses seem pleased with this state of affairs, and do not respond well to the idea that they prefer a mere narcotic to "the real thing." But most important is that mass culture seems to absorb the energies which might be directed toward social revolution, the creation of a better society. Since the narcotic of popular culture short-circuits the effort to establish a socialist society, the theorists of mass society condemn popular culture as "escapism." Shils remarks on the historical significance of such a stand: "Nothing shows the persistence of puritanical Marxism in the writings critical of popular culture as much as the idea that popular culture is 'escapist.' Underlying it is the belief that man's first obligation is to understand his environment in order to transform it into the socialist society. Expressive dispositions, the need for phantasy, the play of imagination, are disregarded by this standpoint. The same hostility against 'art for art's sake' which was characteristic of Marxist literary criticism reappears here in another guise and context."[4]

Where previously the cruelties and vagaries of "the system" accounted for the "crisis in culture," now it is the result of modern industrialism itself, mass culture, which threatens high culture. In a strange unanimity with critics on the political Right, the theorists of mass society decry the effect of mass culture on the creative minorities. The disintegration of the creative elites—a theme developed at length by Karl Mann-

[4] *Ibid.*, p. 592.

heim—is taken up by Dwight MacDonald, who has now come full circle from Trotskyism to an elitism which, as he has recently acknowledged,[5] is hardly to be distinguished from that of T. S. Eliot. But this was only to be expected, if the lines we have traced in the intellectual history of the 19th century are relevant, for a unifying element among the theorists of mass society, Right or Left, is their elitism and their opposition to the liberal tradition. Their conception of the good society is not "the open society" but a *Standesgesell-schaft*, a hierarchy in which intellectuals occupy a special position. As John Fisher has pointed out in a review of *Mass Culture*: "For the theory which permeates the collection is essentially European in its origins and its outlook. Its underlying assumptions—usually unspoken, but set forth quite explicitly by Clement Greenberg, Ernest van den Haag, and a few others, might be summed up about like this:

(1) True culture is the product and property of an intellectual elite; it can, therefore, flourish only in a hierarchical society.

(2) In such a society, which has been the European norm for a good many centuries, the intellectual has a special, well-defined and privileged position as the guardian priest of High Culture. An open, mobile and non-hierarchical society such as America's is a Bad Thing because it does not provide this sheltered niche for intellectuals, or accord them the deference and caste-privileges which they regard as their due.

[5] See "Correspondence," *Sewanee Review*, Spring 1958. In his "London Letter," *Encounter*, November 1956, MacDonald attributes the high quality of the best British journalism to the large class gap between this work and the yellow journalism of "the masses." High quality is maintained because the editors and the public can share a universe of discourse at a high level, and are not obliged, as in the United States, to cater to an enormous middle-brow audience. Bernard Rosenberg fails to see the political implications of MacDonald's position in his introduction to *Mass Cutlure*, where in discussing the political alignment of the critics of mass culture, he lumps together as "conservatives" Eliot, Ortega and Canon Bell, and cites Clement Greenberg and MacDonald as "radicals" (*op. cit.*, pp. 3-4). Yet this misleading statement was quoted with tacit approval by the reviewer of *Mass Culture* in the *American Journal of Sociology*, Vol. 62, May 1957.

(3) Whenever the masses touch culture, they inevitably defile it. Moreover, they commit blasphemy, by approaching a holy object without the permission and guidance of the priestly caste.

(4) Whatever is popular is, by definition, bad. It would therefore be a waste of time and a task unworthy of an intellectual to attempt to distinguish between the degrees of badness."[6]

In surveying the same volume of essays, Shils finds that the theorists of mass culture have developed a special image of the ordinary man.

". . . The ordinary citizen who listens to the radio, goes to films and looks at television is not just *l'homme moyen sensuel* known to past ages. He is a 'private atomic subject,' utterly without religious beliefs, without any private life, without a family which means anything to him; he is standardized, ridden with anxiety, perpetually in a state of 'exacerbated' unrest, his life 'emptied of meaning,' and 'trivialized,' 'alienated from his past, from his community, and possibly from himself,' cretinized and brutalized. The ordinary man has, according to this view, been overwhelmed by the great society; he had lost his roots in his organic communities of territory and kinship, craft and faith. . . . Modern man is incapable of having genuinely affectionate relationships with other persons. He can no longer love. Mass culture is welcomed by this unfortunate being because it 'adjusts' him to an unworthy reality by 'helping us to suppress ourselves.' Lacking religion, man can find surcease from his burdens only in the movie theaters."[7]

Of course this desperate view of an atomized culture is countered by an equally extreme idealization of a departed

[6] John Fisher, "The Masses and the Arts," *Yale Review*, Autumn 1957, pp. 114-115.

[7] Shils, *op. cit.*, pp. 596-597. In constructing this composite indictment, Shils cites the work of Horkheimer and quotes from his article, *op. cit.*, pp. 292-294; he quotes Rosenberg, *op. cit.*, pp. 4, 5, 7; Howe, *op. cit.*, p. 498; Erich Fromm, *The Art of Loving* (New York: Rinehart, 1956), pp. 83-106; and Howe, *op. cit.*, p. 497.

golden age. We have already seen the beginnings of this nostalgia in 19th century French conservatism, and even in Marx's concept of idyllic feudal relations. Here it is expressed in terms of culture; in the old *Standesgesellschaft* everybody had his place. There was no mass culture, only the high culture of the aristocrats (and intellectuals) and the "folk culture" of the peasants. There is no problem of vulgarity of taste; there is no problem of "escape." The people in such a society felt none of the dehumanizing pressures, none of the anxieties of modern life. The antecedents for such an image, suggests Shils, are to be found in German sociological romanticism—beginning with Hegel, through Marx and Engels, Tönnies, Simmel, and Sombart—and find their synthesis in the views of the Frankfurt *Institut für Sozialforschung*. The *Institut* was attached to Columbia University during the late 1930's and early 1940's. There it exerted some influence on the group around the now defunct journal *Politics* edited by Dwight MacDonald in the 1940's. Shils cites the latter group as still another source of the critique of mass society.

The most important institutional source of the critique, however, is undoubtedly the Frankfurt *Institut*. As Shils points out: "The Marxism of the *Institut* was never the Marxism of the parties and barricades, and it never felt bound by the arid dogmas of the Marxist parties. In a series of important collaborative works which included *Autorität und Familie* (Paris, 1934), *The Authoritarian Personality* (New York, 1948), and a variety of other equally characteristic books like Fromm's *Escape From Freedom*, Neumann's *Behemoth*, Horkheimer's *Eclipse of Reason*, and most recently Marcuse's *Eros and Civilization*, an ingenious, courageous and unrealistic point of view was promulgated and applied to modern society. A fusion of Hegelian Marxism, psychoanalysis, and aesthetic repugnance for industrial society, each freely and imaginatively adapted to the underlying philosophy of the *Institut*, dominated their point of view."[8]

[8] Shils, *ibid.*, p. 600.

It is possible that Shils has underestimated the intellectual significance of the *Institut*: as a confrontation of Marx and Freud in theory and research, it represents one of the most important schools of social thought in the 20th century. While he criticizes their Marxism, he perhaps does not take sufficient note of the importance of the effort to reconcile the two theories—the hallmark of their work—and to establish—for example in the works of Erich Fromm—a scientific basis for a humanistic ethic which took into account the class analysis of Marx and the important new insights of psychoanalysis. It is difficult to do justice to the impact of a work like *Escape from Freedom*, especially on young social scientists in the United States, many of whom were introduced to an inter-disciplinary approach to social problems through such books. And *The Authoritarian Personality* represents a landmark in the attempt to correlate psychological characteristics and political predispositions. The efforts of these exiles from Naziism, cut off as they were from their own culture, to interpret the events of their century with the tools of social science, often writing in a second or third language, must be regarded as nothing less than heroic. Shils' analysis is fundamentally correct, but could have been tempered with such recognition. His is the first attempt, however, to assess their perspective and probe their basic assumptions.

"The Institut's point of view was formed in its most general outlines in Germany and in the first years of exile in Europe but it developed into a critique of mass culture only after the immigration to the United States. Here they encountered the 'mass' in modern society for the first time. Their anticapitalistic, and by multiplication, anti-American attitude found a traumatic and seemingly ineluctable confirmation in the popular culture of the United States. Whereas in Europe, an educated person of the higher classes could, and even now still can, avoid awareness of the life of the majority of the population, this is impossible in the United States. What is a vague disdain in Europe must become an elaborate loathing in America."[9]

In their efforts to understand what had happened to them and to Germany, these refugee intellectuals might be forgiven the tendency to see totalitarianism lurking around the corner in their new home, the United States. As social scientists, they were obliged to explain why National Socialism had triumphed in a country with a strong working-class movement and dedicated Socialist parties. Marxism could only explain part of the situation: "It might explain why the property-owning classes welcomed National Socialism but it could not explain why there was so much voluntary and enthusiastic submission, on the part of those who might have been expected, on the basis of an attachment to the ideals of liberalism and socialism, to resist. Why had the working classes not been true to the revolutionary vocation with which Marxism had endowed them? Here German romanticism, brought up to date by sociology and psychoanalysis, appeared to offer an answer."[10]

In the effort to understand the historically decisive failure of the German working classes to resist Hitler, the refugee intellectuals explained the phenomenon in terms of facts perceived from the standpoint of their values. They concluded that the "defection" of the German working classes was due to their alienation and rootlessness within modern mass culture.

"It was because man was alienated and uprooted that he so eagerly accepted the cruel and spurious ethnic community proffered by National Socialism. The same factors which lead them to National Socialism are responsible for modern man's eager self-immersion into the trivial, base and meretricious culture provided by the radio, the film, the comic strips, the television, and mass-produced goods. It is therefore to be expected that the mass culture which has been created to meet the needs of alienated and uprooted men will further the

[9] *Ibid.*
[10] *Ibid.*, p. 601.

process, exacerbate the needs and lead onto an inevitable culmination in Fascism."[11]

If Shils' analysis is correct here, it helps explain the pre-occupation of these *émigré* intellectuals with mass culture: for in it they saw the beginnings of the most traumatic event of their lives and possibly of their century—the rise of Naziism in what had been one of the most civilized countries in the world.

Perhaps the most serious charge of the theorists of mass society against mass culture is that it prepares the way for totalitarianism. Totalitarianism is viewed as the inevitable result of a vacuum in the realm of the spirit, the secularization of society which was part of the program of liberalism. The theorist of mass society regards this vacuum as being filled by mass culture, with dire consequences in the political realm.[12] The fact that Soviet totalitarianism did not emerge out of such a process, and that, as Shils notes, "Fascism triumphed in Germany, Italy and Spain before the 'masses' in these and other countries began to enjoy the benefits of mass culture" does not give pause to the theorists of mass society. Is it possible that they are generalizing from a single set of historical experiences, guided by *a priori* assumptions which do not fit other cases.

Theories may be put to the test of logical consistency, and it is to this end that I should like to compare two works mentioned by Shils, *The Authoritarian Personality*[13] and *Eros and Civilization*.[14] I wish to discuss their portrait of the mass man, and the role of the family within that "mass culture" which

[11] *Ibid.*

[12] These ideas were given a classic sociological expression by Karl Mannheim in *Man and Society in an Age of Reconstruction, op. cit.*, and *Diagnosis of Our Time* (London: Routledge, Kegan Paul, 1943); and of course by Ortega in *The Revolt of the Masses, op. cit.*, although the argument is not so clear cut as in the work of other theorists of mass society—e.g., Fromm's *Escape from Freedom, op. cit.*

[13] T. W. Adorno, Else Frenkel-Brunswick, D. J. Levinson, R. N. Sanford, et al., *The Authoritarian Personality* (New York: Harper, 1950).

[14] Herbert Marcuse, *Eros and Civilization* (Boston: Beacon Press, 1956).

leads to totalitarianism. The superimposition of Freudian theory on Marxism, together with elements of romanticism and existentialism, may produce theoretical difficulties from within; indeed, the definition of the mass man itself may suffer shifts of content which are difficult to reconcile with scientific method.

One of the benchmarks of this school of mass society theorists is that with few exceptions they are ready to consider aspects of life in the United States and Great Britain as "totalitarian." This use of the term is extremely confusing in that, in the effort to assess common trends and similarities, it manages to fudge the distinction between a police state and a politically liberal society. Conventional definitions of this term tend to stress its more narrow, political meaning. Thus, a recent authoritative study declares that "totalitarian dictatorship is historically unique and *sui generis*."[15] The authors go on to define what they consider to be the six basic features of totalitarian dictatorships: "The 'syndrome,' or pattern of interrelated traits, of the totalitarian dictatorship consists of an ideology, a single party typically led by one man, a terroristic police, a communications monopoly, a weapons monopoly, and a centrally directed economy. Of these, the last two are also found in constitutional systems: Socialist Britain had a centrally directed economy, and all modern states possess a weapons monopoly."[16]

Some theorists of mass society, however, feel that such a definition does not do justice to the similarities of these countries to Nazi Germany, Soviet Russia, and Communist China. The difficulties of adducing the same causes in the rise of totalitarianism under such different circumstances has been cited in connection with Arendt's analysis. However, many of these theorists of mass society employ a specifically psychological approach to social life and politics. Without resolving the problems which arise out of a combination of

[15] C. J. Friedrich and Z. Brzezinski, *Totalitarian Dictatorship and Autocracy* (Cambridge: Harvard University Press, 1957), p. 5.
[16] *Ibid.*, p. 9.

Freudian and Marxian theory, they acknowledge the importance of economic and historical factors, declare that it is impossible to study everything, and point out that the psychological sphere is somehow more immediate, or at least mediates between, the influences emphasized in the more orthodox Marxist approaches.[17] In the case of such studies as *Autorität und Familie*[18] and *The Authoritarian Personality*, the emphasis was on the connection between authoritarianism and fascism—thus, both implicitly and explicitly, the importance of a specific psychological type in the rise of totalitarianism.[19] It is not my purpose here to evaluate the methodology or the results of *The Authoritarian Personality* studies. This has been competently done elsewhere.[20] Rather, I should like to take note of the kind of family structure and the personality type emerging from it, which, in the view of the Berkeley group, is influential in the rise of totalitarianism.

From the Freudian perspective, the family is of fundamental importance as the primary group within which socialization of the child takes place. The authors of *The Authoritarian Personality* declare that the interrelationships of parents, children and siblings are of paramount importance in determining their future political activities.[21] The authors distinguish different kinds of family relations for their extremely prejudiced and extremely unprejudiced respondents. (We will leave aside the question of whether there is any intrinsic connection between ethnic prejudice and totalitarianism.) Preju-

[17] Else Frenkel-Brunswick, "Interaction of Psychological and Sociological Factors in Political Behavior," *American Political Science Review*, 46, 1952.

[18] Max Horkheimer (ed.), *Studien über Autorität und Familie* (Paris: Alcan, 1936).

[19] Else Frenkel-Brunswick, "The Role of Psychology in the Study of Totalitarianism," C. J. Friedrich (ed.), *Totalitarianism* (Cambridge: Harvard University Press, 1954).

[20] Richard Christie and Marie Jahoda, *Studies in the Scope and Method of the Authoritarian Personality* (Glencoe: Free Press, 1954). Jahoda, a sympathetic critic, declares that critical analysis has suggested that "empirical evidence is obtained and used only to bear out the researchers' theoretical position assumed before they started the study and not modified after the effort." *Ibid.*, p. 19.

[21] *Ibid.*, p. 385.

diced, "authoritarian" subjects reported a harsh, threatening home discipline. Clearly defined roles of dominance and submission in interpersonal relationships characterized these subjects' family life, as well as a demand for great conformity, lack of spontaneity, lack of mutuality, and great moral indignation on the part of the parent, subsequently internalized by the child. The reaction of hostility from the child is often transformed, through guilt and identification with the aggressor, into rigid glorification and idealization of the parental figures. The prejudiced subjects tended to identify with the strong and to have contempt for the weak; to idealize rugged masculinity and to strive compensatorily for independence. This kind of family situation I will refer to as the authoritarian family ideal. The typical products of such families are regarded by the authors as possessing character structures most vulnerable to the appeals of totalitarianism.

The unprejudiced subjects, on the other hand, came from families where the attitude of the parents tended to be less demanding, more loving and spontaneous, with less concern over status and "proper" behavior. As there was less surrender to conventional rules, relations within the family tended to be more individualized and there was more unconditional affection granted the children. Condemnation was replaced by an attempt to provide guidance and support, which helped in the long run to foster self-reliance. This complex led, according to the authors, to a richer emotional life. They appear to be describing a child-centered atmosphere similar to that of the "progressive" school—and I will refer to this kind of family as the progressive family pattern. The products of such families are regarded as being, to a great extent, free of ethnic prejudice and immune to the blandishments of totalitarianism.

Now the basis for these ideal types was already established in the work of Erich Fromm in *Autorität und Familie*, as well as his *Escape from Freedom*, and in the work of Wilhelm

Reich.[22] Both Fromm and Reich are specifically credited by the authors as having influenced their thinking on authoritarianism.[23] Reich is particularly instructive in that he explicitly tries to unite Marxist and Freudian theory with a series of analogies between the layers of character structure and the class strata of society. Character structure is a trichotomous affair; the first layer, an outer superficial one of social co-operation, where the individual is "restrained, polite, compassionate and conscientious," Reich calls a "false, sham-social surface." The second, which is referred to as consisting of "cruel, sadistic, lascivious, predatory and envious impulses," is the Freudian unconscious, which "orgone biophysics" has shown to be a secondary result of the repression of primary biological impulses. By penetrating this layer, one comes to the third, "the biological core." "In this deepest layer, man, under favorable social conditions, is an honest, industrious, cooperative animal capable of love and also of rational hatred." The romanticism involved in this formulation is not absent in *The Authoritarian Personality*; it is simply not made explicit. Reich's integration is formulated as follows: "We can now apply our insights into human structure to the social and political field. It is not difficult to see that the diverse political and ideological groups in human society correspond to the various layers of human character structure. We do, of course, not follow idealistic philosophy in its belief that this human structure is eternal and unalterable. *After social conditions and changes have formed the original biological needs into the character structure, the latter, in the form of ideologies, reproduces the social structure.*"[24]

On the basis of this interpretation, Reich constructs a theory of mass man and mass society in which each layer of society corresponds to one of the divisions in the character structure: "In this characterological sense, 'fascism' *is the basic emo-*

[22] Wilhelm Reich, *The Mass Psychology of Fascism* (New York: Orgone Institute Press, 1946).
[23] *Ibid.*, p. 231.
[24] *Ibid.*, p. 20.

tional attitude of man in authoritarian society, with its machine civilization and its mechanistic-mystical view of life. It is the mechanistic-mystical character of man in our times which creates fascist parties, not vice versa. . . . Fascism as a political movement differs from other reactionary parties in that it is *supported and championed by masses of people. . . .*

"In contradistinction to liberalism, which represents the superficial character layer, and to genuine revolution, which represents the deepest layer, fascism represents essentially the econd character layer, that of the secondary impulses. . . . In its pure form, fascism is the sum total of all *irrational* reactions of the average human character. . . . Today it has become absolutely clear that fascism is not the deed of a Hitler or a Mussolini, but the expression of *the irrational structure of the mass individual. . . . Fascist mysticism is orgastic longing under the conditions of mystification and inhibition of natural sexuality.*"[25]

The image of the mass man projected by Reich is definitely reflected in *The Authoritarian Personality* studies. The movement of the German middle classes and many German industrial workers toward the Right instead of the Left in the late twenties and thirties is interpreted by Reich as evidence that "sexual inhibition alters the structure of the economically suppressed individual in such a manner that he thinks, feels and acts against his own material interests." Unlike the authors of those studies, however, he advocates a specific political goal which follows from his premise that "the mechanism which makes the masses of people incapable of freedom is the social suppression of genital love life in children, adolescents, and adults."

"The practical problem of mass psychology, then, is that of activating the passive majority of the population which always carries political reaction to victory; and the elimination of the inhibitions which counteract the will to freedom as it is generated by the socio-economic position. If the psychic energies

[25] *Ibid.,* pp. 22-23.

of the average mass of people watching a football game or a musical comedy would be diverted into the rational channels of a freedom movement, they would be invincible."[26]

For Reich as for the Berkeley group and the early Fromm, the mass man is rigid, molded in the authoritarian family with its tremendous demands for conformity. He is sexually anxious and inhibited, ready to idealize the totalitarian demagogue as the authoritarian father he has already internalized, prejudiced and aggressive toward minority groups— the most recent victims in a long chain, the first of which were his own impulses.

I will not raise the question of whether this ideal type could be successfully transplanted and superimposed, as it were, over elements of the American middle class, political ideologies and all. The Leftist bias in *The Authoritarian Personality* studies has been competently analyzed by others.[27] The uncritical application to American data of concepts developed on the basis of European materials and conditions is not a novelty in American sociology. What I wish to emphasize here is the unusual contrast in the conception of the family context and childhood training of the "mass man" as revealed in a comparison of the above view with that of another mass society theorist, Herbert Marcuse. This contrast is especially striking because of the broad similarities of perspective among these theorists of mass society. Marcuse and others have developed a conception of the family background and personality structure of the individual ripe for the appeals of totalitarianism which is quite contradictory to that of the Berkeley group. Totalitarianism, far from being viewed as a consequence of the authoritarian family pattern, is viewed instead as a result of the *decline* of this pattern.

[26] *Ibid.*, pp. 24-25.

[27] Christie and Jahoda, *op. cit.*; cf. especially the essays by Herbert H. Hyman and Paul B. Sheatsley. "The Authoritarian Personality—A Methodological Critique," and Edward A. Shils, "Authoritarianism: 'Right' and 'Left,' " *ibid.*

"The technological abolition of the individual is reflected in the decline of the social function of the family. It was formerly the family which, for good or for bad, reared and educated the individual, and the dominant rules and values were transmitted personally and transformed through personal fate. . . . Through the struggle with father and mother as personal targets of love and aggression, the younger generation entered societal life with impulses, ideas, and needs which were largely *their own*. Consequently, the formation of their superego, the repressive modification of their impulses, their renunciation and sublimation were very personal experiences. Precisely because of this, their adjustment left painful scars, and life under the performance principle still retained a sphere of private nonconformity."[28]

Now, however, Marcuse sees the instincts as being prematurely socialized by "a whole system of extra-familial agents and agencies," including the instruments of mass culture: "As early as the pre-school level, gangs, radio and television set the pattern for conformity and rebellion; deviations from the pattern are punished not so much within the family as outside and against the family. The experts of the mass media transmit the required values; they offer the perfect training in efficiency, toughness, personality, dream and romance. With this education, the family can no longer compete. In the struggle between the generations, the sides seem to be shifted; the son knows better; he represents the mature reality principle against its obsolete paternal forms. The father, the first object of aggression in the Oedipus situation, later appears as a rather inappropriate target of aggression. His authority as a transmitter of wealth, skills, experiences is greatly reduced; he has less to offer, and therefore less to prohibit. The progressive father is a most unsuitable enemy and a most unsuitable 'ideal'—but so is any father who no longer shapes the child's economic, emotional and intellectual future."[29]

This is clearly a plea for an authoritarian family pattern,

[28] Marcuse, *op. cit.*, p. 96.   [29] *Ibid.*, p. 97.

as against a more progressive type. In spite of all the evidence offered, for example, by the Berkeley group as to the consequences of an authoritarian family milieu, and the literary evidence in the bitter recollections of such critics of Victorian family life as Samuel Butler, in Marcuse we are confronted by a mass society theorist who declares that the patriarchal, authoritarian family inculcates norms and standards without which the individual falls prey to mass culture and totalitarianism. The individual is seen as being left without any real object for his rebellion, his natural aggression, in the "normal" resolution of the Oedipal conflict.[30] Since there is no real father in the family, and by Reichian analogy, no real exploiter in the economic system (the place of the latter having been taken by clean-shaven, smiling bureaucrats) the introjected guilt is turned against the self. The ego of the individual "has shrunk to such a degree that the multiform antagonistic processes between id, ego and superego cannot unfold themselves in their classic form."[31] This free analogy from psychological structure to social structure and back again not only assumes a tacit norm in the "classic" Oedipal resolution, but also offers as a social analogue of the conflict of father and son another "resolution" in the relation between a (presumably) oppressed proletarian class and its bourgeois exploiters. The analogue of Oedipal aggression is clearly social revolution, the "freedom movement" of Reich.

Our primary interest here, however, is in the contrast between Marcuse's analysis and that of the Berkeley group. Certainly the inability of the child to "idealize" the more progressive father because of the latter's easy-going attitudes would not be bemoaned by them as it is by Marcuse. His whole line of analysis appears to be directly contradictory to the work of the early Fromm and the Berkeley group with regard to the authoritarian, oversteered and overdisciplined victims of the German patriarchal family. Their Freudian-

---

[30] *Ibid.*, pp. 96-97.
[31] *Ibid.*, p. 99.

Marxist analyses have thus produced opposite conclusions. Both of these family types with their characteristic products cannot be important influences in the rise of totalitarianism, yet they are both subsumed under the rubric of "mass society" in these theories. The oversteered authoritarian and the "loose" progressive type are both identified as the "mass man."[32]

In the contrasting images of the kind of person who is most vulnerable to the appeals of totalitarianism, a difficulty of Freudian explanation appears which Freud himself recognized.[33] Psychoanalytic explanation is usually of a *post factum* character. Both the Berkeley group and Marcuse reflect this, particularly in that aspect of their work which seems to be rationalistically derived from prior premises rather than the result of empirical inquiry. Part of the problem is in the Hegelian legacy—the dialectical use of words with shifting meanings, so that it may be difficult at any given time to determine which meaning is involved. Thus the use of the concept of "totalitarianism" to describe societies as different as the United States and Nazi Germany quickly reaches a point of diminishing returns: to describe the causes of something is difficult enough without changing the "something" to be explained. The same is true of concepts like "mass man" and "mass society."

[32] In addition, Marcuse is involved in a contradiction within his own theory. Although he takes the position that the authoritarian father must be retained in order to allow the "normal" or "classic" Oedipal resolution to take place and provide a focus for aggression which relieves guilt, he quite paradoxically visualizes a future ideal society in which a disintegration or withering away of the family would occur. (*op. cit.*, pp. 201ff.) It is this latter aspect of Marcuse's philosophy, together with the assumption that advocacy of sexual freedom is inevitably associated with political radicalism, which has been labelled "instinctivist radicalism" by Dr. Fromm in their debate in the quarterly *Dissent*. See Erich Fromm, "The Human Implications of Instinctivistic 'Radicalism,'" reprinted in *Voices of Dissent* (New York: Grove Press, 1959), pp. 313-320. This debate shows the lines of the split between the Left and Right wing among mass society theorists, based on the interpretation of Freud rather than Marx.

[33] *Collected Papers*, II, pp. 226-27. Cited by Philip Rieff, "History, Psychoanalysis and the Social Sciences," *Ethics*, Vol. 63, January 1953.

The analysis of the mass man, the product of mass culture who becomes the potential totalitarian, leads to contradictory images from similar premises. Such a contradiction may indicate that the relation between psychological type and political predisposition has been too loosely drawn. It is quite possible that different class levels—e.g., within German and American society—are being tapped in this research and theory, with different classes being regarded as the "typical." Thus a theory based originally on the German lower-middle class may have been generalized to the American "middle class" by the Berkeley group:[34] whereas Marcuse seems to regard the "other-directed" man as the norm for American culture. It is difficult to see how both of these "types" could be held responsible for the rise of totalitarianism in the ordinary political sense of that word. These contrasting theories, however, may also have resulted from extra-scientific judgments which guided them from the beginning and inevitably influenced their outcome. To the role of such judgments in social science inquiry we now turn.

[34] Adorno, *et al., op. cit.*, p. 23: "The findings of the study may be expected to hold fairly well for non-Jewish, white, native-born, middle-class Americans."

CHAPTER SEVEN

SUBJECTIVITY IN SOCIAL RESEARCH

CONFRONTED with the foregoing analysis, a critic might conceivably put the following question: even if the theorists of mass society are animated in their approach by a transmuted Marxism, does this not leave open the question as to whether their analysis is in fact correct?[1] In short, given a certain bias, a certain perspective on contemporary life, what is there which prevents their analyses from being valid?

Writing in another context, Shils himself has recognized this problem. On the basis of the following quotation, he might perhaps be indicted for a failure to practice what he preaches: "However there is a characteristic outlook closely connected with this doctrine (that a truth is true with reference to the social position and outlook of those who hold it) which has gained widespread acceptance in our society as well as in unfree countries, and is consequently much more dangerous. I refer to the view that, in examining the statements made by historians or other students of society, it is more important to lay bare the influence of personality, or of class, or political affiliation, than it is to examine the truth of what they are asserting. That seems to me to be a very widespread view. It is found in almost every learned journal in the social sciences throughout the Western world. This is a dangerous view because it rests on the assumption that the political sphere is more important than the intellectual sphere."[2]

It is impossible not to sympathize with Shils' dilemma here. I shall try to provide him with a hypothetical rejoinder against the accusation, made against him not only by others but also by himself, that by concentrating his fire on the social

[1] This question is raised by Louis Coser, "Daydreams, Nightmares, Professor Shils," *Dissent*, Summer 1958.

[2] Edward Shils, "Discussion," *Science and Freedom: Proceedings of the Hamburg Congress* (Boston: Beacon Press, 1953), p. 174.

and political philosophy of the mass society theorists, he is ignoring the question of the validity of their analysis.

American social scientists, historians and political scientists are almost unanimous in proclaiming a hard and fast distinction between values and facts, between the origins of a proposition and its validity.[3] This view is even shared by practicing sociologists of knowledge; indeed, it has become an accepted axiom in the field. Yet there is something about such an assertion which, in the social sciences at least, fails to satisfy. The large ideological and subjective element in sociological conceptualization is one reason for this. Gunnar Myrdal has commented brilliantly, for example, on this problem in the work of American sociologists of the second generation: "The presence of this . . . static and fatalistic valuation in the hidden ethos of contemporary social science is suggested by some of the terminology found throughout the writings of many sociologists, such as 'balance,' 'harmony,' 'equilibrium,' 'adjustment,' 'maladjustment,' 'organization,' 'disorganization,' 'accommodation,' 'function,' 'social process,' and 'cultural lag.' While they all . . . have been used advantageously to describe empirically observable situations, they carry within them the tendency to give a do-nothing (*laissez-faire*) valuation of those situations."[4]

It is all very well to insist that the world may be neatly divided into realms of fact and realms of value, but in the

[3] See for example, Talcott Parsons, *The Structure of Social Action* (New York: McGraw-Hill, 1937), pp. 431-438; George H. Sabine, "Logical and Social Studies," *Philosophical Review*, Vol. 48, 1939, pp. 155-176; Robert K. Merton, "The Sociology of Knowledge," *Social Theory and Social Structure* (Glencoe: Free Press, 1949); Hans Speier, "The Social Determination of Ideas," *Social Research*, Vol. 5, 1938, pp. 182-205; Talcott Parsons, review of Alexander von Schelting, *Max Weber's Wissenschaftslehre* (Tubingen, 1934), *American Sociological Review*, Vol. 1, No. 4, August 1936, p. 675; Gerard de Gré, "Sociology of Knowledge and the Problem of Truth," *Journal of the History of Ideas*, 2, 1941, pp. 110-115; and Maurice Mandelbaum, *The Problem of Historical Knowledge* (New York: Liveright, 1938), pp. 193-194.

[4] Gunnar Myrdal, "A Methodological Note on Facts and Valuations in Social Science," *An American Dilemma* (Harper: 1944), p. 1056. Myrdal acknowledges the influence and assistance of Arnold Rose in the preparation of this Appendix.

social sciences it is easy to demonstrate that these realms touch and interpenetrate. Myrdal has done so in economics and sociology in his excellent *Methodological Note* and elsewhere.[5] Anthropologists are confronted with similar problems. For example, J. W. Bennett has suggested that the "objective" interpretations of Hopi and Zuni culture by anthropologists are influenced by two diametrically opposed value-orientations contained within the leading concepts and approaches employed, resulting in conflicting interpretations.[6] The society of these Pueblo Indians "has been described by certain well-trained anthropologists as highly integrated, and their typical personality as gentle, cooperative, modest and tranquil. Other well-trained anthropologists have described the same people as marked by hidden tension, suspicion, anxiety, hostility, fear and ambition. Now it seems to some of us that these different accounts result from the approval the first anthropologists gave to the moral unity of Pueblo life, and from the disapproval the second group of anthropologists gave to the authoritarianism and repression of Pueblo society. It appears that both accounts are true."[7] "The social scientific research," declares Bennett rather modestly, "may have been directed and influenced in part by personal-cultural differences between the respective workers, and not merely by the division of scientific labor."[8] But it should not astonish us that social science research should be influenced by the character and cultural background of the social scientist. This could only be shocking to the positivist for whom science had become the New Jerusalem. The human qualities of the sociologist and the anthropological field worker are among his basic research tools. Without them he would be helpless. Unlike the chemist

[5] For example, in his *Political Element in the Development of Economic Theory* (London: Routledge, Kegan Paul, 1930).

[6] J. W. Bennett, "The Interpretation of Pueblo Culture: A Question of Values," *Southwestern Journal of Anthropology*, Vol. 2, No. 4, Winter 1946.

[7] Robert Redfield, *The Little Community* (Uppsala: Almqvist and Wiksells, 1955), pp. 136-137.

[8] Bennett, *op. cit.*, p. 364.

in the laboratory, the field worker is himself one of the mole-cules he is studying. It is through knowing himself that he comes to know others.

But it is not only in sociology and anthropology that this situation prevails. Psychology too is influenced by the per-sonalities of psychologists. In a recent assessment of the field, the author declares that "different perspectives in personality theory seem to be in part projections—e.g., the product of the author's personal and cultural orientations as well as the data on which they are presumably based."[9] ". . . Trying to formu-late a personality theory is very much like trying to read meaning into an ambiguous stimulus. We have very little available in the form of 'hard facts' or 'systematic knowledge' and yet we try to read meaning into what is available in a perfectly natural desire to make sense as we go along. But as in all projection, the result reflects as much our own mo-tives and values as it does the 'facts' objectively 'out there.' "[10]

McClelland cites examples from among the co-authors of the volume containing his essay. He distinguishes the French appreciation of conceptual clarity and rationality, Anglo-Saxon readiness to employ concepts or hypotheses pragmatically so long as they provide a means to continue inquiry, German preference for polarities, hierarchical models, and intuitive understanding of others. And he makes the point that all of these emphases represent quite characteristic ways of think-ing about the world which are common in these different cultures as they have been described by anthropologists and other students of national characteristics. As an example of the general differences between European and American theories of personality taken as a whole, the author of a summary article in the same volume suggests that the following descrip-tion has at least "a kernel of truth" though he rejects it as being too broad: "Shall we then say that by and large Ameri-

[9] David C. McClelland, "Toward a Science of Personality Psychology," in Henry P. David and Helmut von Bracken (eds.), *Perspectives in Per-sonality Theory* (New York: Basic Books, 1957), p. 356.
[10] *Ibid.*

can theorists view personality in terms of outer behavior, surface attributes, motor components, interpersonal relations, and modifiability? Do Europeans, by contrast, adhere to concepts of deep dispositions, constitutional determination, structural firmness, relative independence of society, and therefore relative unmodifiability?"[11]

Statements like these indicate that a sociology of knowledge for the social sciences, though lacking precision, can point a methodological lesson. This lesson indicates that a doctrine of segregation regarding facts and values, rigidly applied in sociology, may be quite unrealistic. And in the case of the theorists of mass society, it has shown us the extent to which the very concepts, the key distinctions and terms used by these theorists, are the bearers of a certain kind of intellectual freight.

How has the problem of fact and value been dealt with in American sociology up to now? The first generation, as we have seen, were social reformers like Ward, Ross or Small, or old-fashioned liberals like Sumner, who promoted their particular version of the natural-law fallacies discussed in the first chapter. Fact and value were merged, and the methodological issue had not yet been sharply defined. This was the work of the second generation, who in their sincere striving to achieve the status of "scientists," repudiated at least overtly the reforming spirit of the founding fathers. This group was also interested in reform, but their positivistic zeal led them to distinguish between their efforts as scientists and their duties as citizens. Fact and value were sharply separated. But as some astute critics were to realize, and as some of the second generation must have realized themselves, their ban on values only forced their value-judgments underground. This only made it necessary to smuggle them back into their work by other means. This tendency was roundly condemned by a third group, students of the "scientific generation," whom I

[11] Gordon W. Allport, "European and American Theories of Personality," *ibid.*, p. 5.

144

shall call the revisionists. These men were exposed to European social theory and imbibed, along with their Weber, neo-Kantian theories of knowledge; and with their Marx and Mannheim, a feeling for the problems of ideology in sociology itself. Thus men like Louis Wirth, Robert MacIver and Robert S. Lynd confronted the fact-value problem as a real issue which the "scientific" generation had mishandled. They were encouraged in this by their more open interests in the need for reform and value-oriented sociology, best exemplified in Lynd's famous *Knowledge for What*.[12] The revisionists accused their intellectual fathers of a combination of innocence and dishonesty in separating the realms of fact and value. They detected a *laissez faire* bias in the work of their mentors which, aside from its practical implications, was also not even good "science." So Gunnar Myrdal, who, though not an American, belongs to this group, was led to comment on the way in which values had become entwined in the concepts of American sociologists of the second generation.[13] Myrdal's plea was, in effect, for a more reform-minded sociology in which inevitability would not be built into the conceptual scheme and the possibility of amelioration would be admitted. This program suffered, however, from a number of defects. Myrdal did not consider the problem that a sociology oriented toward amelioration might present: the problem that it was itself "biased" in the direction of change. The revisionists generally refused to give up the positivism which they had absorbed from the second generation. They continued to utilize the framework of "science," and with it the radical distinction between facts and values. They did not stop to ask themselves whether a sociology which was biased in the direction of change was any more "scientific" and less normative than a sociology biased in the direction of equilibrium. And the program of the revisionists, aimed at eliminating the static bias which they thought they detected in the work of the

[12] Robert S. Lynd, *Knowledge for What?* (Princeton: Princeton University Press, 1939).
[13] Myrdal, *op. cit.*

second generation, called for an extremely simple-minded solution: we must declare our biases on the first page of our sociological studies, and then we can assimilate them to the positivist canon. This act of avowing one's biases on page one is perhaps comparable in the effectiveness of its ritualism to the incantations of Indians praying for rain. The revisionists did not stop to consider the possibility that it might not be so easy to "reveal" one's biases, or that, once revealed, they might not cease to affect the objectivity of the research.

The solution to this hoary problem which I am about to offer may be no solution at all. Nor can I associate it with a generation, as I cannot presume to speak for my own. In the first place, it is axiomatic that values cannot be derived from science—from "facts." Vestiges of this kind of natural-law thinking remained even in the work of the revisionists. The effort to pull "what ought to be" out of an analysis of "what is" should be abandoned. Our values must stand on their own feet, and should not expect pseudo-supports from the social sciences. So far as the influence of social and political philosophies on conceptualization and research, we may be faced with the problem of redefining their role. Subjective factors in research should be viewed from a rather different standpoint than in old-fashioned positivism. In the human sciences, it is very often precisely the prejudices and the biases of the observer which lead him to certain problems, which cause him to structure his analysis in a certain way, and which allow him to see what he does see and what he tries to report. We should try to take this into account in any philosophy of the social sciences. And yet we must do this without relinquishing the humility of the scientific enterprise, the emphasis on confirmability of theories by other investigators, the effort to test our formulations wherever and whenever this is possible, the dedication to the ideal, at least, of impartiality. This is obviously no easy task, and yet the situation in the social sciences seems to call for a reassessment of the role of subjective factors in research. Myrdal's effort to define the role of values in conceptualization resulted in a position very close to the one here presented.

"Many scientists attempted to avoid . . . biases by choosing new terms for the same things which do not carry such apparent connotations of valuation. This attempt is in our view misdirected. Biases are not so easily eradicated. And in this case they signify—though in a concealed and therefore uncontrollable way—valuations necessary for the setting of scientific problems. 'Without valuations,' Professor Louis Wirth writes, 'we have no interest, no sense of relevance or of significance, and, consequently, no object.'

"The value-loaded terms have a meaning and represent a theoretical approach, because the theoretical approach itself is determined by the valuations in the governing *ethos* of a society. When this is seen clearly, and when those valuations are made explicit, and consequently, *the terms are defined in relation to the valuations*, then, and only then, are we in the position to use the terms freely without constantly endangering the theoretical analysis by permitting biases to slip in. There is thus no sense in inventing new scientific terms for the purpose. New terms for old things can only give a false security to ourselves and bewilder the general public. In the degree that the new terms would actually cover the facts we discussed in the old familiar terms—the facts which we *want* to discuss, because *we are interested* in them—they would soon become equally value-loaded in a society permeated by the same ideals and interests. Scientific terms become value-loaded because society is made up of human beings following purposes. A 'disinterested social science' is, from this viewpoint, pure nonsense. It never existed and it will never exist. We can make our thinking strictly rational in spite of this, but only by facing the valuations, not by evading them."[14]

[14] *Ibid.*, pp. 1063-1064. Myrdal's later views of this problem, which represent an extension and development of his statements above, have recently been published in an American edition together with the original essays in *An American Dilemma*. See Paul Streeten (ed.), *Value in Social Theory* (New York: Harper & Bros., 1959).

This position should not be seen as leading to a completely subjectivist anarchy in the social sciences. The social scientist is still under the obligation to be as "objective" as possible— i.e., to try to establish intersubjectively verifiable criteria for checking his generalizations where possible, and to avoid wilful distortion. This is somewhat consonant with the Weberian canon. But it includes the obligation to avoid disguising value judgments as facts. This view has been expressed recently by a perceptive student of theories of social disorganization. After reviewing a large number of approaches to the field, the author concluded that the study of social problems required a normative social theory, and that the presentation of normative formulations disguised as empirical statements resulted only in confusion. His conclusion was that value-premises, far from being undesirable, were necessary for significant and effective research. On the contrary, the disguising of value judgments as facts, a common occurrence in the theories under review, was singled out as undesirable and unrealistic.

"The theory of social problems cannot assume efficient form unless it is recognized for what it is—a judgmentally normative social theory. Moreover, so long as we admit the legitimacy of alternative value structures, we must recognize that there is no *single* theory of social problems, but many *theories* of social problems. Meanwhile, insofar as the theories of social problems are of a normative rather than an empirical type, they are outside the province of the scientist as scientist. As a scientist, one can apply one's knowledge to any given set of goals, demonstrating (1) whether they are attainable; (2) if so, how they can be most efficiently attained; and (3) what the consequences of attaining them may be. However, as a scientist one cannot prescribe goals.

"Thus the peculiar adolescence of this particular field, its tendency to blow hot and cold by turns, its sudden embarrassments and hollow pretensions—these, it is maintained, are due to the attempt to cast contradictory role requirements in a single mold. It has been the peculiar destiny of thinkers in this field to search for a single solution to social problems— as if there were only one—and to seek scientific objectivity under conditions where it was in principle impossible."[15]

Values are functional for social scientists just as they are for the people whom social scientists study. Most sociological studies, with the possible exception of those which are really historical and descriptive, such as collections of census materials and demographical surveys, but possibly even including these, will be shaped in their presuppositions, methods, problems and concepts by social and political philosophies. A "pure science" of the type which sociologists, clinging to Newtonian imagery, imagine to be carried on by the physicist, is hardly possible in the social sciences, nor is it even desirable. Whatever is achieved will be achieved by virtue of certain perspectives; and our perspectives allow us to see certain things and overlook others. It might be argued that some perspectives are better than others. But the Olympus from whose heights we might choose among world-perspectives in a conclusive way is not to be found in this world.[16] A liberal who believes

[15] Don Martindale, "Social Disorganization," H. Becker and A. Boskoff, *Modern Sociological Theory* (New York: Dryden, 1957), pp. 366-367.

[16] See Kasimir Ajdukiewicz, "The Scientific World-Perspective," in H. Feigl and W. Sellars, *Readings in Philosophical Analysis* (New York: Appleton, Century, Crofts, 1949), p. 188: "Thus there would stand over and against one another two opposed judgments of the truth of a world-perspective. Now the epistemologist takes upon himself the role of an impartial umpire. To which of the two world-perspectives shall he concede the advantage with respect to truth? Is, however, the epistemologist truly an impartial umpire? Is he not also imprisoned in a conceptual apparatus which dictates to him his world perspective? Even the epistemologist cannot speak without a language, cannot think without a conceptual apparatus. He will thus make his decision as to truth in a way which corresponds to his world-perspective.

"The epistemologist therefore is not suited for the role of an impartial umpire in the struggle between two world-perspectives for the title of truth. Consequently, he should not push forward to assume this role. Instead of this he should set himself another task. He should give his attention to the changes which occur in the conceptual apparatus of science and in the corresponding world-perspectives, and should seek to ascertain the motives which bring these changes about. Perhaps this sequence of world-perspectives permits of being conceived as a goal-directed process which advances

in the desirability of a multiplicity of points of view will not be too saddened by this state of affairs. Social scientists may find it possible to agree on intersubjectively verifiable criteria of evidence. But the historically transcendent guarantee for certainty lies outside the domain of the social sciences.

It may be easier to test some theories than others, because some are more easily reducible to simple operational terms. Unfortunately those theories which are of the greatest general interest, like the theory of mass society, are not of this type. History is a laboratory, as John Stuart Mill said, but not one which permits much in the way of precise controls which would allow us to test for the significance of the presence or absence of a factor, holding other conditions constant.[17] That this should be the fate of some of the most interesting ideas concerning social and political development, however, should not cause undue dismay. The problem is one of expecting the precision of the chemistry laboratory in a field where such precision is not available. Where it *is* available, alas, the studies which it is possible to carry out do not often lend themselves to broad application. They are often "valid" only for the particular situation in which they are tested, or they have relevance only for a very limited range of social behavior and not for the broader movement of social and historical forces.

What shall be the final judgment on the work of the theorists of mass society in the light of these observations on method? Does not the declaration of methodological tolerance

---

as though someone consciously wished to achieve the goal by means of the sequence. The task involved in such a conception of the history of science constitutes the sound kernel of the *geisteswissenschaftlichen* understanding of the evolution of science."

[17] Comparative historical study can yield approximations of this type. For example, Hartz's interpretation of American political and social thought in terms of the absence of a prior feudalism, and his explanation of the failure of socialism in the United States, represents such an approximation. But because of the presence and absence of a large number of other factors in the two situations—the one broadly "European" and the other equally broadly "American"—the "testing" really permits of very little control.

also extend to them? Yes, I would say, in the sense that they see what they do by virtue of their conceptual framework. But their judgments of the quality of modern life—as well as their scientific statements as to the effects of industrialization and democratization—must be read with an awareness of the intellectual orientation from which they spring, which is only to say that the former have no scientific guarantee, since none is in principle possible; and that the latter must be subjected to the same patient inquiry and attempts at independent confirmation which is their due. But where valuations are disguised as facts, this will substantially affect a scientific theory. It is this particular defect which informs the theory of mass society.

One may entertain values without deriving them from "science" or hiding them behind terms like "rationality." Social science studies carried out from the standpoint of such values will be influenced by them, to be sure. The values will have facilitated the study and the discovery involved. But then the question arises as to the "scientific" validity of such studies. If their conclusions are confirmed by other investigators, then the fact that the study was informed by certain values is less important. This will be less true, of course, if the confirmation comes from students with similar values. Intersubjectively confirmable truth can still be subject to the limitations of collective ignorance. Thus in the time of Ptolemy, the consensus of the competent was that the sun rotated around the earth. But there appears to be no way of avoiding this problem, except to make provision for continuity of inquiry, leaving the door open for new approaches. Even if value judgments are inevitable in research, in short, we must maintain some procedure for distinguishing between varying degrees of adequacy of belief. Independent confirmation by other observers, so important in some natural sciences, is clearly limited in many branches of the social sciences. The insight of perspectivism, that no single human can know the whole truth about his society, applies also to human social scientists. But instead of trying to claim a guarantee such as the one Karl Mannheim claimed for the intellectuals as to the validity of their insights, we should acknowledge the extent to which acceptance of "truth" in social science is determined in part by an agreement among social scientists as to the warrantability of beliefs. And we should perhaps acknowledge that it is in the nature of social science that it may be influenced in its methods and results by the character of the observer. I have labored this point because I believe that the positivistic dictum concerning subjectivity—that it must be extirpated root and branch—has passed its period of usefulness in some areas of the social sciences. Many sociologists are still clinging to methodological notions concerning "science" which have been questioned by scientists for decades.[18]

Perhaps I have not here provided a solution to the problem posed by the hypothetical critic of Shils, and by implication, of my own work. By showing that the line between facts and values in the social sciences is not as sharp as a positivistic generation believed, however, I have tried to indicate that studies of the intellectual orientation of a student of society, his social and political beliefs—not to speak of his character and his culture—will be important for the understanding of his research, and, in cases in which values are disguised as facts, as a basis for an evaluation of it. In the analysis of mass culture carried out by the mass society theorists I do not quarrel with many of the statements they make about the quality of much of popular culture. My quarrel is with their contention that their theory is the result of a purely scientific analysis,[19] with their presumed scientific judgment of the relation between mass society and totalitarianism, and by im-

[18] The views presented here find support in two recent contributions by prominent philosophers of science. See Michael Polanyi, *Personal Knowledge*, (London: Routledge, Kegan Paul, 1958); and P. W. Bridgman, "Remarks on Niels Bohr's Talk," *Daedalus*, Spring 1958, p. 175.

[19] Marcuse may be exempted here in that he explicitly declares his work to be a "philosophy of psychoanalysis" rather than a contribution to psychoanalysis itself. But he accepts Freud's thought as a scientific basis from which to derive implications for his philosophy and his utopia.

plication, of the results of industrialization and democratization. From the standpoint of a different set of values, one could also say, for example, that ". . . much of what is so repugnant in contemporary culture is a crude manifestation of a quickened imagination, a heightened responsiveness, of a search for experience; it is an effort to live outside the constrictions imposed by poverty, tradition, and authority."[20] It is not my purpose here to argue the merits and deficiencies of popular culture, or to debate the social and political advantages of extensive dissemination of "high culture" downwards and the creation of a vast middle-brow group in the United States.[21] I merely wish to indicate that different kinds of theories concerning "mass society" could be developed on the basis of values different from those of the theorists of mass society. And on the problem of subjectivity in social research, I can do no better than to quote the anthropologist Robert Redfield, who spoke for many others when he said:

"In me, man and anthropologist do not separate themselves sharply. I used to think I could bring about that separation in scientific work about humanity. Now I have come to think that it is not possible to do so. All the rules of objectivity I should maintain: the marshaling of evidence that may be confirmed by others, the persistent doubting and testing of all important descriptive formulations that I make, the humility before the

[20] Edward Shils, "Correspondence," *Sewanee Review*, Spring 1958, p. 357.

[21] I have not treated the work of such liberal defenders of popular culture as David Riesman, Gilbert Seldes, Lyman Bryson, Jacques Barzun (in earlier books), David Manning White, and others; but even these, as Shils notes, spend most of their time criticizing the opponents of popular culture for being undemocratic or unrealistic. They themselves are not too enthusiastic about the content of much of the popular fare of the mass media, though Riesman once held the view that it was possible to reach personal autonomy through leisure rather than through work. Most of their arguments are based on the increasing dissemination of high culture throughout the population and the variety of cultural possibilities available to hitherto underprivileged groups. Cf. for example, Daniel Bell, "The Theory of Mass Society," *Commentary, op. cit.*, p. 81; and such representative works of Riesman as the articles in Section IV, "Culture: Popular and Unpopular," *Individualism Reconsidered, op. cit.*

facts, and the willingness to confess oneself wrong and begin over. I hope I may always strive to obey these rules. But I think now that what I see men do, and understand as something that human beings do, is seen often with a valuing of it. I like or dislike as I go. This is how I reach understanding of it. The double standard of ethical judgment toward primitive peoples is a part of my version of cultural relativity. It is because I am a product of civilization that I value as I do. It is because I am a product of civilization that I have both a range of experience within which to do my understanding-valuing and the scientific disciplines that help me to describe what I value so that others will accept it, or, recognizing it as not near enough the truth, to correct it. And if, in this too I am wrong, those others will correct me here also."[22]

[22] Robert Redfield, *The Primitive World and its Transformations* (Ithaca: Cornell University Press, 1953), p. 165.

SELECTED BIBLIOGRAPHY

Adorno, T. W., et al. *The Authoritarian Personality*. New York: Harper, 1950.

Adjukiewicz, Kasimir. "The Scientific World-Perspective," in H. Feigl and W. Sellars, *Readings in Philosophical Analysis*. New York: Appleton, Century, Crofts, 1949.

Allport, Gordon W. "The Historical Background of Modern Social Psychology," in Gardner Lindzey (ed.), *Handbook of Social Psychology*. Cambridge: Addison-Wesley, 1953.

————. "European and American Theories of Personality," in Henry F. David and Helmut von Bracken (eds.), *Perspectives in Personality Theory*. New York: Basic Books, 1957.

Arendt, Hannah. *The Origins of Totalitarianism*. New York: Harcourt, 1951.

Bauer, Raymond and Alice H. "American Society and the Mass Media of Communication," (mimeographed), *Journal of Social Issues*, 1961 (forthcoming).

Becker, Carl. *The Heavenly City of the 18th Century Philosophers*. New Haven: Yale University Press, 1938.

Bell, Daniel. "The Theory of Mass Society," *Commentary*, July 1956.

Blumer, Herbert. "Moulding of Mass Behavior Through the Motion Pictures," *Publications of the American Sociological Society*, Vol. 29, 1935.

————. "Collective Behavior," in A. M. Lee (ed.), *Outlines of Sociology*. New York: Barnes and Noble, 1946.

————. "Collective Behavior," in J. P. Gittler (ed.), *Review of Sociology*. New York: Wiley and Sons, 1957.

Bottomore, T. B., and Rubel, M. (eds.), *Karl Marx: Selected Writings in Sociology and Social Philosophy*. London: Watts, 1956.

Brinton, Crane. *The Anatomy of Revolution*. New York: Prentice Hall, 1938.

Christie, Richard, and Jahoda, Marie. *Studies in the Scope and Method of the Authoritarian Personality*. Glencoe: Free Press, 1954.

Coser, Lewis. *The Functions of Social Conflict*. Glencoe: Free Press, 1956.

Friedson, Eliot. "Communications Research in the Concept of the Mass," *American Sociological Review*, Vol. 18; reprinted in W. Schramm (ed.), *Process and Effects of Mass Communication*. Urbana: University of Illinois, 1955.

Fromm, Erich. *Escape from Freedom*. London: Routledge, Kegan Paul, 1942.

Hallowell, John A. *The Decline of Liberalism as an Ideology*. London: Routledge, Kegan Paul, 1946.

Hardman, J. B. S. "Masses," *Encyclopedia of the Social Sciences*. New York: Macmillan, 1935.

Hartz, Louis. *The Liberal Tradition in America*. New York: Harcourt Brace, 1955.

Hayek, F. A. *The Counter-Revolution of Science*. Glencoe: Free Press, 1952.

Hinkle, Roscoe C., Jr., and Gisela J. *The Development of Modern Sociology*. Garden City: Doubleday, 1954.

Hofstadter, Richard. *Social Darwinism in American Thought*. Boston: Beacon, 1955.

————. *The Age of Reform*. New York: Knopf, 1955.

Hughes, H. Stuart. *Consciousness and Society: The Reorientation of European Social Thought, 1890-1930*. New York: Knopf, 1958.

Karpf, Fay B. *American Social Psychology: Its Origins, Development and European Background*. New York: McGraw-Hill, 1932.

Katz, Elihu, and Lazarsfeld, Paul. *Personal Influence*. Glencoe: Free Press, 1955.

Lazarsfeld, Paul F., Berelson, Bernard, and Gaudet, Hazel. *The People's Choice*. New York: Columbia University Press, 1948.

Le Bon, Gustave. *The Crowd*. London: Ernest Benn, 1947.

Lederer, Emil. *The State of the Masses*. New York: Norton, 1940.

Lippmann, Walter. *Public Opinion*. New York: Macmillan, 1922.

Lynd, Robert S. *Knowledge for What?* Princeton: Princeton University Press, 1939.

Mandelbaum, Maurice. *The Problem of Historical Knowledge*. New York: Liveright, 1938.

Mannheim, Karl. *Diagnosis of Our Time*. London: Routledge, Kegan Paul, 1943.

————. *Man and Society in an Age of Reconstruction*. New York: Harcourt Brace, 1950.

————. "American Sociology," *Essays on Sociology and Social Psychology*. New York: Oxford University Press, 1953.

Marcuse, Herbert. *Eros and Civilization*. Boston: Beacon Press, 1955.

Bibliography

Martindale, Don. "Social Disorganization," in H. Becker and A. Boskoff, *Modern Sociological Theory*. New York: Dryden, 1957.

Marx, Karl, and Engels, Friedrich. *Manifesto of the Communist Party*. Chicago: Charles H. Kerr, 1940.

Mill, J. S. "On Liberty," *Utilitarianism, Liberty and Representative Government*. New York: Dutton, 1951.

Mills, C. Wright. "The Professional Ideology of Social Pathologists," *American Journal of Sociology*, Vol. 49, No. 2, September 1943.

————. *The Power Elite*. New York: Oxford University Press, 1956.

Moore, Barrington, Jr. "Sociological Theory and Contemporary Politics," *American Journal of Sociology*, Vol. 61, No. 2, September 1955.

Myrdal, Gunnar. "Appendix 2: A Methodological Note on Facts and Valuations in Social Science," *An American Dilemma*. New York: Harper, 1944.

Nisbet, Robert A. "Conservatism and Sociology," *American Journal of Sociology*, Vol. 18, No. 2, September 1952.

————. "The French Revolution and the Rise of Sociology," *American Journal of Sociology*, Vol. 49, No. 2, September 1943.

————. *The Quest for Community*. New York: Oxford University Press, 1953.

Ortega y Gasset, José. *The Revolt of the Masses*. New York: Pelican, 1950.

Page, Charles H. *Class and American Sociology: From Ward to Ross*. New York: Dial, 1940.

Park, Robert E., and Burgess, E. W. *Introduction to the Science of Society*. Chicago: University of Chicago Press, 1921.

Park, Robert E. "The City: Suggestions for the Investigation of Human Behavior in the Urban Environment," *American Journal of Sociology*, March 1915.

————. *Human Communities*. Glencoe: Free Press, 1952.

————. *Society*. Glencoe: Free Press, 1955.

Redfield, Robert. *The Primitive World and Its Transformations*. Ithaca: Cornell University Press, 1953.

Reich, Wilhelm. *The Mass Psychology of Fascism*. New York: Orgone Institute Press, 1946.

Riesman, David. *Individualism Reconsidered*. Glencoe: Free Press, 1954.

Riesman, David. *The Lonely Crowd*. New York: Doubleday, 1953.

Rose, Arnold. "The Concept of Class and American Sociology," *Social Research*, Vol. 25, No. 1, Spring 1958.

Rosenberg, Bernard, and White, D. M. *Mass Culture*. Glencoe: Free Press, 1956.

Salomon, Albert. *The Tyranny of Progress*. New York: Noonday Press, 1955.

Shanas, Ethel. "The Nature and Manipulation of Crowds," Unpublished M.A. thesis, University of Chicago, Department of Sociology, 1937.

Shils, Edward A. *The Present State of American Sociology*. Glencoe: Free Press, 1948.

——. "Daydreams and Nightmares: Reflections on the Criticism of Mass Culture," *The Sewanee Review*, Vol. 65, No. 4, October-December 1957.

Shklar, Judith. *After Utopia*. Princeton: Princeton University Press, 1957.

Simmel, Georg. *The Sociology of Georg Simmel* (ed. by Kurt H. Wolff) Glencoe: Free Press, 1950.

Sprott, W. H. J. *Science and Social Action*. Glencoe: Free Press, 1956.

Sumner, William Graham. *Folkways*. Boston: Ginn and Co., 1906.

Sumner, William Graham. "Sociology," in Perry Miller (ed.), *American Thought*. New York: Rinehart, 1954.

Wirth, Louis. "American Sociology, 1915-1947," *American Journal of Sociology*, Index to Vols. 1-52, 1895-1947.

Wolff, Kurt H. "Notes Toward a Socio-Cultural Interpretation of American Sociology," *American Sociological Review*, Vol. XI, 1946.

Zetterberg, Hans L. "A Guide to American Sociology, 1945-55," *Sociology in the United States of America*. Paris: UNESCO, 1956.

INDEX

Index

industrialization, 33, 35n, 36, 75, 79, 91, 97, 122-23, 151, 153
Inkeles, A., 112n
Institut für Sozialforschung, 126-29

Jahoda, Marie, and Christie, Richard, 131n, 135n
James, William, 60
Jaspers, Karl, 34n, 40n
Jennings, Herbert S., 90n

Kahl, Joseph, 3n
Karpf, Fay B., 52n, 58
Katz, Elihu, and Lazarsfeld, Paul, 98, 106n
Kendall, P. L., and Lazarsfeld, P. F., 104n
Khrushchev, Nikita, 112
Killian, Lewis M., and Turner, Ralph H., 58n
Klapper, Joseph T., 105
Knowledge for What, 145
Kramer, M., 13n, 24n
Krikorian, Y., 78n

Larrabee, Harold A., 78n
Lasswell, Harold D., and Lerner, Daniel, 97n
Lazarsfeld, Paul F., 103; and Katz, Elihu, 98n, 106n; Berelson, Bernard, and Gaudet, Hazel, 100n; and Stanton, 101n; and Kendall, P. L., 104n
LeBon, Gustave, 42n, 52n, 53-57, 59n, 62, 64
Lederer, Emil, 41-43
Lee, A. M., 57n
"Left" politics, 16, 28n, 41n, 50, 74, 134-35; and critique of liberalism, 18, 124; and theory of mass society, 34, 43, 121-22, 124, 138n
Lenin, Nikolai, 37
Lerner, Daniel, 112n, 115; and Lasswell, Harold D., 97n
Lewin, Kurt, 98
"liberal," 16n
liberalism, 4n, 134; in American sociology, 17, 21, 49-50, 57, 70, 91-92, 95, 112-13; opposition to, 16-18, 29, 34, 40-41, 43, 53-59, 70, 71n, 95, 121, 124, 128-29;

and theory of mass society, 30, 36-38
Lichtenberger, J. P., 79
Lindzey, Gardner, 55n, 56n
Lippmann, Walter, 58n
Locke, John, 12, 14, 50n
Lockwood, David, 23n
Lowenthal, Leo, 121n
Lumsdaine, Arthur A., Hovland, Carl I., and Sheffield, Fred D., 110n
Lunt, Paul S., and Warner, W. Lloyd, 98n
Lynd, Robert S., 93, 145

McClelland, David C., 143
Maccoby, E. E., 104n
MacDonald, Dwight, 121n, 124, 126
McDougall, William, 52n, 53n, 55-56
MacIver, Robert M., 22n, 93, 145
McKenzie, Roderick D., 88
Madge, John, 3n
Maine, Sir Henry, 31-32
Maistre, Joseph de, 11, 13-14, 17, 19, 24-25
Mandelbaum, Maurice, 141n
Mannheim, Karl, 35, 37, 40-41, 49, 51, 69, 70, 101n, 123-24, 129n, 145, 152
Marcel, Gabriel, 34n, 40n
Marcuse, Herbert, 126, 129n, 135-39, 152n
Martin, Everett Dean, 59
Martindale, Don, 74, 88-89, 149n
Marx, Karl, 17, 21, 25, 28, 30n, 32, 36-37, 40, 42n, 77-78, 123, 126-27, 138n, 145. *See also* Marxism
Marxism, 21-22, 36, 41-43, 50, 63, 70, 78, 90n, 91n, 108, 118, 122-23, 126-28, 130-31, 133, 138, 140
"mass," concept of the, 27-30, 34n, 35n, 36n, 37-40, 42-43, 55n, 62, 64-65, 67-68, 101n, 104-05, 108, 113, 122-25, 127, 129. *See also* crowd and mob
mass behavior, 57n, 63-68, 103. *See also* collective behavior
mass media of communications,

Index